the Working woman's

woman's

From baby's room
to boardroom —
you can have it all!

Baby planner

Marla Schram Schwartz

Published by Sourcebooks, Inc.
P.O. Box 4410, Naperville, Illinois 60567-4410
(630) 961-3900
FAX: (630) 961-2168
www.sourcebooks.com

Originally published in 1993 by Prentice Hall

Library of Congress Cataloging-in-Publication Data

Schwartz, Marla Schram.
  The working woman's baby planner / Marla Schram Schwartz.
    p. cm.
  Includes index.
  Originally published: Englewood Cliffs, N.J. : Prentice Hall, c1993.
  ISBN 1-4022-0554-6 (alk. paper)
  1. Pregnant women—Employment. 2. Pregnancy. 3. Mothers—Employment. 4. Child care. I. Title.

HD6055.S34 2005
331.4'4—dc22
                                                    2005017680

Printed and bound in the United States of America.
VHG 10 9 8 7 6 5 4 3 2 1

Table of Contents

Acknowledgments

I would like to thank all the people who have contributed to *The Working Woman's Baby Planner*. I am deeply indebted to those who instructed me, reviewed sections of the book, and provided technical as well as moral support. They include: my first literary agent, Irv Settel, who believed in this project years before it finally sold; my current agent, Alison Picard, who enthusiastically helped resell it; my helpful and friendly editor, Deborah Werksman; Loretta Hess, for helping me put this book together; Dr. Robert Braun, Dr. Albert Schwartz, Dr. Michael Hemsley, Dr. Kenneth Spaulding, Dr. Ken Cosmer, and Dr. Raymond Poliakin and his nurse Crystal Davidson, for their time, generosity, and instrumental medical editing; Karen Schwartz and Michelle Hazlewood, certified fitness instructors, for their prenatal exercise and nutritional guidelines editing; Joel Framson, CPA, for his budgeting and insurance expertise; the many working women who took the time to share their employment, pregnancy, and childbirth experiences with me; Dinah Braun Griffin and Sara Lynn Mandel, my dear friends, for critiquing my manuscript; Maria Sanchez, for helping me to care for my children so I could complete the manuscript; my daughter, Lindsey Erin, and my son, Brendan Taylor, who constantly inspired me by saying, "Mommy, when are you going to finish your book?"; and for my always supportive husband, Arnie. A special dedication to my mother, Elaine Schram, who taught me from a very early age that not only can women do anything they set their minds to, but they can do it and raise happy families at the same time.

I would also like to thank the many people, companies, organizations, associations, support groups, and agencies for all their assistance. My deepest appreciation goes to the many incredible people, both inside and outside the health profession, who have contributed to improving the quality of pregnancy and childbirth. I hope my book expresses their concerns while offering expectant working women an up-to-date view of the art and science of this field. If I have left anyone out, it was not intentional, and your information was truly valuable to the compilation of my book.

Introduction

As a pregnant working woman, you face the special challenge of meeting the demands of your job and your pregnancy without compromising either one. *The Working Woman's Baby Planner* will show you how you can remain effective and professional on the job while taking care of all the personal—and often intrusive—needs that accompany pregnancy.

The *Planner* takes you through the complete cycle of this important time in your life, from early pregnancy to your return to work. It addresses virtually every one of your concerns as a pregnant working woman from relieving physical discomforts at work, to eating for two on a busy schedule, to understanding relevant labor laws, to negotiating your maternity leave.

Dozens of practical, easy-to-follow tips and strategies are provided for dealing with these concerns, as well as the unique issues you face, such as telling your boss that you're pregnant, understanding your coworkers' reactions, and maintaining your professional appearance as your pregnancy progresses.

One of the special features of the *Planner* is its ready-to-use format. Time-saving worksheets, checklists, and charts are included throughout the book to provide you with valuable tools for organizing your busy life at home and at work.

Since more than 75 percent of working women return to their jobs before their child's first birthday, an entire section of the *Planner* has been devoted to the critical issue of child care. Here you will find all the tools and information you need to make the right child-care choices for you and your family, and to make your transition back to work as smooth as possible. Alternative work ideas are also outlined for the many burned-out working moms such as creating nontraditional schedules, starting your own business, or telecommuting.

As a first-time mother-to-be, I found working through my pregnancy particularly rough because I didn't know to whom to turn or what to expect. I read many childbirth books, but they all had one fundamental problem: they did not address the unique concerns of the pregnant woman who works throughout her pregnancy. I needed a book that would help guide me in my quest to successfully combine my work with pregnancy and motherhood. I hope *The Working Woman's Baby Planner* answers that need for you.

I sincerely hope in the future our society will become more sensitive and responsive to the needs of working mothers. For now, the best way I have found to achieve the quality of life you are working toward is to enjoy your job, share your concerns and hopes with others, be loving to your mate, patient with your child, and flexible with your life.

Every Happiness!

Marla Schram Schwartz

Part One

Prenatal Care on the Job

Chapter 1

Minimizing Physical Discomforts

Although most working women experience healthy, normal pregnancies, it's difficult not to feel uncomfortable at times. Many of these discomforts are annoying rather than being any real cause for alarm. You are likely to find commuting more stressful, you may be suffering from morning sickness which can be quite draining, and you may find being on your feet for long periods very tiring.

Start by pinpointing problem areas and adapt your routine to accommodate your pregnancy. You can help to stay comfortable by exercising regularly and drinking plenty of water throughout your nine months. "Plenty" means eight to ten glasses every day—about two quarts. Try a sparkling variety or squeeze a little fruit into your glass to liven up the taste. If commuting is difficult, ask if you can come in later and leave later. If you are tired after work, don't be hard on yourself—domestic chores can wait. Ask for help from your partner with things like cooking and cleaning. Working long hours during pregnancy, particularly in a physically demanding job, can reduce fetal growth, so for this reason alone you should carefully consider your options.

How to Remain Professional When You're Not Feeling Well

Here are a few general tips on how to remain professional if you find yourself not feeling well or if you're too uncomfortable to continue activities that involve coworkers:

- Try to sit near the door at all meetings—formal and informal—so you can slip out unobtrusively should the need arise.

- If you're in a small meeting and cannot slip out, always excuse yourself and leave, rather than suffering through the meeting. If you stay, you'll be unable to concentrate, your coworkers will probably notice that something is wrong, and you may disrupt the meeting. While most coworkers will understand, some will not. Always be as professional as possible. If you're giving a presentation, use this as an opportunity to take a short breath. Tell your coworkers to take a minute to grab a cup of coffee, stretch, and so forth.

- Keep a box under your desk, and if possible, put your feet up while working. Wear comfortable clothing and shoes.

- Always be prepared. Keep an "emergency kit" with supplies in your desk. The chart on page 21 will provide you with a complete list of what you might need.

Strategies for Coping with Common Discomforts

The following are the most common pregnancy concerns and the strategies to deal with them while you are on the job:

Backache

Backaches are common during pregnancy because of the increased weight you're carrying, especially if your baby is resting on your spine. Neck and shoulder aches can be due to tension and/or the increased weight of your growing breasts. Lower back pain that extends or shoots down one buttock and into one leg is probably sciatica, caused when the baby's head compresses the sciatic nerve. The tips that follow will help to relieve the discomfort of backaches or avoid them altogether:

- *Drive comfortably*—Move your car seat forward to keep your knees bent and higher than your hips. Use a small pillow to support your lower back area.

- *Lift correctly*—Stabilize your body first by assuming a wide stance and tucking in your buttocks. Bend at the knees, not at the waist, and lift with your arms and legs, which will take the stress off your back. Lift objects only chest high. If your job demands frequent heavy lifting, ask to be assigned to less taxing duties.

- *Limit your standing*—Try not to stand in one place or one position for too long. If your job requires long periods of standing, keep one foot on a raised surface, such as a step or a box, to prevent your lower back from curving inward; or stand on a small, skid-proof rug. When standing at a table, lean forward with your knees slightly bent, and support your weight with your hands or elbows.

- *Use ice or a cold pack*—Place a bag with ice, wrapped in a towel, against the small of your back when you're sitting down.

- *Relieve strain*—When seated at your desk, prop up one leg on a footstool, stack of files, trash can, or anything else available. When walking, sitting, or lying down, avoid putting stress on your back muscles by tucking in your buttocks. Keep your back from arching forward when you stand or lie on your side. At work or at home, you can also lean forward in a chair and lower your head to your knees for thirty seconds. Rise and repeat six times, up to six times a day.

- *Stretch daily*—Try setting the clock on your computer to beep at you every thirty minutes to remind you to stretch.

- *Avoid wearing high heels to work*—Wear sturdy shoes, with a heel no higher than one inch. Save higher heels for special meetings and appointments with clients, and place thin, foam-rubber inserts in the toes to reduce pressure.

- *Wear a maternity belt*—A wide, soft, supportive elastic band that wraps around your lower back and under your belly can take over part of the job of tired, stretched abdominal and back muscles as it cradles the weight of your growing belly.

- *Poor posture can also cause your back to ache*—Try to keep your shoulders and hips in line as you walk, and keep your back straight by tucking a pillow behind you when you're seated.

Edema (Swelling)

More than 70 percent of pregnant women experience some fluid accumulation in their feet, legs, face, and hands. This condition is related to hormone buildup in your system, which results in the kidneys collecting more water and salt than normal. If your job keeps you on your feet, you are also more likely to experience edema.

If you experience sudden, extreme swelling, you should immediately alert your physician. This could be a warning sign of preclampsia or toxemia. Mild swelling, which is considered normal and beneficial, can be relieved by these methods.

- *Raise your legs*—Prop up your legs at work on anything available: a stack of papers, books, or a box. Also, elevate your feet and hands above your heart to reduce swelling by gravity. If possible, lie down during the day on your left (heart) side, not on your back. This position prevents your uterus from compressing major arteries and lets your system reabsorb the fluid. Also try walking around the block on your lunch hour (see "Keeping Fit at Work," page 50).

- *Soak your feet*—Tired, burning feet should be soaked at the end of a workday. Rotate your ankles to reduce swelling.

- *Keep water at your desk*—Consuming extra water will help to draw fluid from puffy tissues back into your bloodstream to be excreted by your kidneys later. Have a glass or a squeeze bottle of water nearby throughout the day.

- *Wear loose clothing*—Although you always want to look well dressed at work, choose looser clothes for maternity wear. Wear elastic support hose, too, and remove tight-fitting rings and other jewelry. Keep an extra, larger pair of shoes in your office to wear when your feet swell.

- *Watch your diet*—Stay away from fatty foods, eat plenty of protein, and cut down on salt, which causes fluid retention.

- *Avoid chemicals*—Chemical diuretics have been found to be harmful to a pregnant woman. Try taking a couple of spoonfuls of apple-cider vinegar, a natural diuretic, before each meal. Herbal and homeopathic remedies can help.

Fatigue

During your first trimester, you may experience extreme fatigue. By the second trimester, your body will probably have adjusted, and you may feel full of energy. By the third trimester, however, you may feel exhausted again and need more rest. There's no cure for this; your body is just reflecting the strains being put on it. These are things you can do to help combat work fatigue:

- *Retire early*—Never mind the undone chores you see all around you. Read "Sleeping Well and Working Refreshed" on page 23, and get to bed.

- *Try to reduce worrying*—Making an effort not to worry about work and home concerns can relieve the tension that builds up during the day.

- *Delegate responsibilities*—If you're in a position to delegate responsibility when the pressure becomes too great, do so. Most coworkers will understand and be cooperative, so don't feel guilty about doing it.

- *Learn your daily rhythms of alertness and fatigue*—Do your strenuous or creative work during alert times; rest during tired periods. Take a short nap every day during your lunch hour. If you don't have a room to retire to, rest your head on your desk or find an empty conference room or lounge you can use. If possible, ask your employer to reduce your hours temporarily if you just can't keep up near the end of your term.

- *Combat anemia*—Anemia can result in tiredness, weakness, and fainting. Add more iron-rich foods to your diet, such as lentils and green leafy vegetables. Doctor-recommended iron tablets can help as well.

Headaches

Headaches are extremely common during pregnancy. They may be caused by hormonal changes over which you have little control. But you may alleviate the problem by doing the following:

- *Rest*—Sit in a dark, quiet room with your eyes closed. Try meditation, yoga, or other relaxation techniques until it passes (see "On-the-Job Stress Reducers and Relaxation Techniques," page 64).

- *Breathe fresh air*—Avoid stuffy, overheated, smoke-filled rooms. Step outside, if possible, for a breath of clear air.

- *Eat regularly*—Little or no food over a long period causes your blood sugar level to drop. Excessive caffeine can cause headaches as well.

- *Try to reduce stress*—Whenever possible, avoid unnecessary stressful situations and find ways to control the stress you cannot avoid.

- *Take calcium*—Calcium tends to quiet your nerves and ease a headache. If the headaches are regular, take up to four 450-milligram calcium tablets a day. If you suddenly develop a severe headache, call your doctor. It could indicate the onset of toxemia.

- *Cut down on your salt intake*—Especially during pregnancy, too much salt can cause headaches and high blood pressure.

- *Use cold compresses*—Place a cold, moist cloth on your forehead or on the back of your neck. Add a few drops of essential oil of lavender on your washcloth.

- *Use liniments*—Rub peppermint oil, Tiger Balm, or white flower oil into your temples, or drink peppermint tea.

- *Take nonaspirin pain relievers*—Get your doctor's approval first.

Heartburn and Indigestion

The heart has nothing to do with this problem, which was named long before it was understood. Heartburn involves regurgitation of stomach acid back into the throat or esophagus. It's a mild form of indigestion that, once again, is caused by your hormonal changes. You may experience a burning sensation in your upper abdomen or lower chest, a bitter taste in your mouth, and belching. Here are ways to relieve this problem:

- *Eliminate certain foods*—Stop drinking citrus fruit juices or beverages made from them. Eliminate rich, greasy, and spicy foods from your diet. Instead, take snacks to work, such as yogurt and honey, papaya, apples, or toast. Also stay away from caffeine-filled drinks.

- *Eat small amounts regularly rather than a few big meals* —Avoid eating too much, too quickly.

- *Drink water*—A glass of water will wash away the acid. Then drink a little milk, buttermilk, or cream to coat your stomach. Or try some peppermint tea.

- *Chew gum*—Chew a stick of gum after meals or sip a carbonated drink.

- *Try a tablespoon of honey in a glass of warm milk.*

- *Use antacids*—Ask your physician about using Maalox or Gelusil to relieve the discomfort. These are products you can keep in your desk drawer and use whenever necessary without disrupting your work. Liquid antacids are more effective than tablets.

- *Change your position*—Try sitting or standing. Avoid lying down; it may only worsen the condition. Sleep propped up with extra pillows—an elevated head may help.

- *Remain upright after eating.*

- *Try some herbal and homeopathic remedies.*

Hemorrhoids

Constipation and straining to move your bowels may cause hemorrhoids (varicose veins of the rectum caused by pressure). While hemorrhoids are common in pregnancy, they shrink right after delivery. If they cause you pain at work, try the following aids:

• If you sit for long hours, use a pillow or a rubber doughnut-shaped cushion to relieve the discomfort. Apply ice packs or pads soaked in witch hazel or Annusol. Drugstores sell Tucks, which work well too.

• If you stand for long hours at work, take sitting breaks whenever your supervisor gives you the okay.

Muscle Cramps

Muscle cramps in the back, groin, and legs caused by slow blood circulation and pressure on certain nerves are common occurrences. If you cramp up at work, give these ideas a try:

• Change your position by sitting in another position for a few minutes.

• If you're standing when the cramp occurs, keep your weight evenly distributed and flex your knees. Avoid pointing your toes. Instead, bring your toes upward, pushing out with your heel.

• Place a hot-water bag or heating pad directly on the cramped muscle.

• Drink lots of fluids. Place two tablespoons of honey in a glass of warm water to help your muscles relax.

• Wear support hose to help relieve leg cramps. A well-fitting maternity girdle and low-heeled shoes will relieve the strain on your muscles as well.

Nausea, Vomiting, and Morning Sickness

Many women suffer from occasional nausea because of the pressure on organs and the high levels of estrogen in the body, especially in early pregnancy. If you are prone to vomiting, keep towels, a trash can, and mouthwash or breath mints at your desk, and figure out the quickest way to the bathroom. If you are driving, have a big bottle of ice water handy and drive with the window down or with cool air on your face. Keep plastic grocery bags ready. There are steps you can take to fend off nausea, among them:

• *Eat little but frequently*—Get plenty of protein. Keep high carb foods like dry crackers, pretzels, popcorn, and toast at your desk. Bananas are nutritious and kind to queasy stomachs.

• *Stay away from coffee and spicy, sweet, or greasy foods*—Add a drop of peppermint oil directly on the tongue or mix with honey. Papaya enzyme and ginger capsules (found in health food stores) are also helpful.

• *Drink carefully*—Drink fruit juices or carbonated drinks at the end of, rather than during, meals. Find out whether very hot or very cold drinks (like ice water) are best for you. Sip on some clove, raspberry, or ginger tea.

- *Try acupuncture*—Wear an acupuncture bracelet found at most stores (e.g., Sea Bands) or apply pressure on your wrist yourself. Gently press on a spot at the center of the underside of your wrist, about three finger-widths below your palm.

- *Use ice*—Bring an ice pack to work. If nausea strikes, fill it with ice and hold it against your forehead or stomach. When an ice bag is not handy, use a cold, moist towel instead.

- *Breathe deeply.*

Nosebleeds

The tiny blood vessels of the nose become more congested during pregnancy and break open easily. That's why nosebleeds are so common. Dry air tends to worsen the problem. You might try these techniques:

- *Apply pressure*—Lean your head forward (not backward, because you could swallow and choke on your blood), and apply pressure to the bridge of your nose with your fingers for at least four minutes. Keep tissues handy on your desk to protect your clothing.

- *Try Vaseline*—Apply Vaseline with a cotton-tip swab to each nostril to stop the bleeding.

- *Use a spray*—If your nose feels uncomfortably full after a nosebleed, mix 1/2 teaspoon of salt with 1/2 cup of warm water, and spray each nostril with the mixture.

Overheating

Your basal metabolic rate (the rate at which you expend energy) increases by 20 percent during pregnancy. This causes sweat glands to work overtime and the blood flow to your skin to increase. You're likely to feel uncomfortable in both warm weather and cold. It will take a little extra effort to keep yourself cool, so try to do the following:

- *Bathe daily*—A daily bath is a must during pregnancy. Also use a good antiperspirant.

- *Dress in layers*—As the office gets warmer, you can remove a layer at a time until you're down to a thin blouse.

- *Keep tissues nearby*—Sometimes sweaty palms make it difficult to work. A box of tissues, a handkerchief, or even a towel are handy things to keep conveniently nearby.

- *Wear foot pads*—If your feet become less tolerant to heat, use foot pads to keep perspiration under control.

- *Keep a fan in your office or at your workstation.*

- *Schedule your time*—Make sure you're not outside between 11:00 and 3:00 when the sun is at its strongest.

- *Try not to accept work assignments that could take too much of a physical toll*—An all-day business conference is draining enough under any circumstances, but for mothers-to-be, such an event can be downright exhausting.

Frequent Urination

Your uterus is placing pressure on your bladder, that's true, but also you're drinking more water to relieve constipation, dehydration, and possibly to treat a urinary-tract infection. To be on the safe side, do the following:

- *Empty your bladder frequently throughout the day*—You may have to explain to your boss that you need more frequent toilet breaks.

- *Wear a sanitary napkin*—Be prepared in case you can't make it to the restroom in time.

- *Tell your doctor*—Frequent urination may also be the result of an infection. If the problem increases, talk to your doctor.

Varicose Veins

When veins become weakened and enlarged because they've had to work harder to circulate the blood, they are called varicose veins. Heredity also plays a part in their development. Pregnant women will often develop them in their legs, and less often, in their genital area. You can expect them to fade dramatically after birth. While you're still pregnant, however, there are efforts you can make to reduce the threat, such as:

- *Move around often*—Walking and exercising provide the best protection against varicose veins. Elevate your legs when you're sitting to hurry the return of blood from your legs.

- *Wear support hose*—Especially if you stand for long periods, wear elastic support stockings or maternity pantyhose, which you should put on while lying on your back. Avoid tight clothing.

- *Don't cross your legs for long periods of time.*

Vision Changes

Increased water retention and elevated hormone levels may cause vision disturbances. The difficulty is only temporary; just take these precautions while waiting for it to pass:

- *Cleanse contact lenses often*—Cloudy contact lenses interfere with your work. Keep a lens-cleaning kit at work and use it whenever necessary. If contacts don't fit as well as usual, wear eyeglasses instead.

- *Use eye drops*—Ask your doctor to recommend a good brand of eye drops and use them several times during the workday.

- *Avoid eye strain*—You may not be able to cut down on reading if your work responsibilities require it. But be sure to rest your eyes in the evening if they've been bothering you. Avoid watching TV.

Creating a More Comfortable Workspace

If you make your workspace as comfortable as possible, you will avoid many of the stresses of working while you're pregnant. Here are easy ways to create a comfortable work environment:

- *Sit in a comfortable chair*—Avoid the back pains that come from sitting long hours by choosing a chair with height adjustment if possible. Set it so that your knees bend at a ninety-degree angle. Rest your feet on a stack of books if you can't adjust the chair. Make sure that the back tilts forward and has a curved backrest that fits to the curvature of your spine. If that's missing, use a throw pillow. Rise from your seat by putting one foot in front of the other, and with a straight back, pushing your hips forward and up.

- *Keep files within reach*—Arrange your work equipment so that you don't have to stretch or bend too much.

- *Keep cool*—Pregnancy will naturally raise your body temperature. Sponge yourself off when you become sweaty and use another application of deodorant. You can also purchase a little battery-operated fan that can attach to your desk to keep you cooler.

- *Avoid unhealthy spaces*—Stay out of smoke-filled rooms. They're not only bad for your baby but they can increase your own fatigue. Stay away from noxious fumes, chemicals, or other hazardous odors. And avoid extremes of temperatures (see "Ensuring Your Safety at Work," page 33).

- *Sit and stand straight*—Whenever you think of it, lift your chest, tighten your stomach muscle, and tilt your pelvis forward. Slumping at your desk, for example, will interfere with your breathing. Make room for your belly when you're seated by keeping your feet several inches apart.

- *Slow down*—This is not the time to go running up stairs or hurrying around the office.

- *Take frequent breaks*—Stand up and walk around after you've been sitting for long periods. Sit down with your feet up if you've been standing for a long time. And lie down on your left side on your lunch hour, if possible. Empty your bladder at least every two hours.

- *Avoid fatigue*—Stop working when you're tired. The more strenuous your job, the more you need to cut down on personal activities and rest whenever you can.

- *Ask your coworkers to help*—Don't be shy about asking for help when you need it. Most coworkers will be happy to oblige.

COMFORT SUPPLIES CHECKLIST

Store these crucial items at your workplace:

- ☐ Tennis shoes or comfortable flat shoes
- ☐ Support hose
- ☐ Sanitary napkins
- ☐ Breast pads
- ☐ Deodorant/antiperspirant
- ☐ Box of tissues
- ☐ Small, battery-operated fan
- ☐ Fruits, vegetables, healthful snack foods, dry crackers, honey, bottled water, and juices
- ☐ Squeeze bottle for water or juices
- ☐ Ice pack and heating pad
- ☐ Wet wipes
- ☐ Lotion or creams for itching and dry skin
- ☐ Doctor-approved medications and vitamins
- ☐ Antacids and gum
- ☐ Acupressure bracelet to help with nausea
- ☐ Toothbrush, toothpaste, and mouthwash
- ☐ A go-with-anything blouse, in case nausea or excessive perspiration gets the better of your clothes
- ☐ Sweater
- ☐ Doctor's and/or midwife's phone number and insurance information

Eating for Two on a Busy Schedule

Eating well while you're pregnant does not have to involve a lot of time and preparation. As a busy working woman, you can make sure that you and your baby are getting all the nutrients you need by creating your own time-saving, easy-to-follow eating plan.

Snacks

Stock your desk and the workplace refrigerator with wholesome snacks, such as plain popcorn, savory crackers, biscuits, cereal/health bars, unsweetened fruit juices, fresh fruits, raw vegetables, whole wheat pretzels, sunflower seeds, seeds or nuts such as almonds or cashews, and of course, the old standbys—plain yogurt and low-fat cheeses. Brush or floss your teeth often because gums are prone to bleeding when you're pregnant.

Nutritious, Quick Breakfasts in Minutes

Many professionals believe that breakfast is the most important meal of the day. Without a good start, you'll have difficulty catching up all day. But a healthy breakfast need not take much time. In fact, some of the meals suggested here may be eaten in your car on the way to work:

- *Quick egg sandwich*—Put scrambled eggs into a pita pocket. Wash it down with orange juice.

- *Cheddar waffles*—Heat two frozen waffles in a toaster oven, topped with a slice of cheddar cheese and black raspberry preserves.

- *Peanut-banana sandwich*—Toast a slice of whole wheat bread and top with peanut butter and sliced bananas.

- *French toast*—Freeze cooked French toast in advance. Thaw in toaster at a light setting, then place cheese and ham between the slices, and heat in toaster oven. Wrap in a paper napkin and bring along a thermos of tomato juice or V8.

- *Apple muffins*—Toast and butter English muffin halves. Spread with applesauce topped with plain yogurt. Sprinkle with wheat germ and cinnamon.

- *Raspberry oatmeal*—Cook one packet of instant oatmeal with milk instead of water and stir in one tablespoon of raspberry fruit spread or jam.

Sleeping Well and Working Refreshed

During pregnancy, it's essential to get the proper rest. That means at least eight hours a night for most people. Moreover, in your condition, you need brief periods of rest on the job if you can possibly arrange it. A nap would be ideal—even for five minutes.

Over the past few decades, scientists have learned that insufficient sleep starves the body of REM (rapid eye movement) sleep, the uninterrupted dreaming that occurs at the end of the sleep cycle. Without it, the psychological restoration that your body requires fails to take place.

The effects of lost sleep begin to accumulate: one night's loss will interfere with your creative thinking, and two nights' loss damages your ability to perform even routine tasks. You become irritable and impatient, you have trouble concentrating, and your interest in sex wanes. If you work with heavy machinery or dispense medication, the potential for mistakes becomes dangerously high.

You can see why the need for adequate sleep is important. You should have the same bedtime every night. In addition, you should exercise regularly in the morning (nighttime exercise may cause insomnia), eat properly, and start preparing for bed as soon as you get home. That may sound strange to you, but if you want to assure a good night's sleep, the process of unwinding begins as you walk through the door. For the first twenty minutes, do absolutely nothing. Then have an early dinner of light, easily digested foods, and a quiet evening.

On-the-Job Energy Boosters

Here are a few things to do that will recharge your batteries:

- *Relax your mind and raise your spirits with a sniff of fragrant oils*—Keep some in your desk and simply place several drops, singly or in combination, on a cloth, in a diffuser, or in a spray bottle.

- *Grab a nap whenever possible (see "Sleeping Well and Working Refreshed," page 23)*—Remove your shoes, loosen your clothes, and lie on your left side. If you can't manage that, find a quiet place and relax with your feet up for a while or rest your head on your arms at your desk.

• *Take a walk*—Find a serene place like a nearby park.

• *Enjoy a quick, nutritional pick-me-up*—Snack on something nutrional; for example, a handful of nuts, peanut butter on a cracker, or a granola bar.

Making Business Travel Easier during Pregnancy

Traveling presents no major problems to most pregnant women, unless you're prone to motion sickness, miscarriages, premature delivery, or if you develop vaginal bleeding. In the first few months, you may find traveling uncomfortable because of the adjustments your body is going through or from morning sickness. The second trimester, generally, is a more comfortable time for business travel. Your body will have made its adjustments and you'll probably be bursting with energy. Once your body becomes bulkier, however, moving around becomes more difficult. And, during the ninth month, you should be close to home or office in case your baby is born earlier than expected.

General Tips for Travel

The Centers for Disease Control and Prevention advises women in their first or second trimester of pregnancy to stay below 4,000 feet above sea level; women in their third trimester should limit their destinations to places no higher than 2,500 feet above sea level. You wouldn't want to risk, for example, the added stress and potential injury of traveling to a remote area where there are no amenities, so be sure to check out water supplies and hygiene levels in the countries you plan to visit.

It's good to carry a copy of your most recent prenatal record, just in case you need to consult another care provider or if you go into labor in a strange city. Research emergency care at your destination (the name and number of someone your healthcare provider recommends, if possible.) You should also make sure that your health insurance is valid while abroad and during pregnancy, and that the policy covers a newborn should you give birth. A supplemental travel insurance policy and prepaid medical evacuation insurance policy should be obtained as well. You should also do the following:

- *Consult your doctor*—You should always check with your doctor if you have any questions about the safety of a proposed trip. Get permission before you take any over-the-counter medication, including motion-sickness pills. Foreign travel will only be a problem if you plan to go somewhere where immunizations are necessary because some (such as typhoid) are dangerous to your baby. Your doctor will advise you about which vaccinations are required and if they are safe for you.

- *Watch your food intake*—Any overeating, or eating greasy, undercooked, or spicy foods, may lead to stomach distress. Carry healthy, energy-boosting snacks in your bag at all times. Eat five or six small meals a day. Don't forget water—now's not the time to become dehydrated.

• *Avoid prolonged sitting*—Staying in one position for long periods, especially cross-legged, will interfere with your circulation. After you've been seated for awhile, rotate your feet at the ankles and walk around.

• *Pack carefully*—Take only what you can carry yourself. Bring along everything listed under the "Comfort Supplies Checklist," on page 21.

• *Be careful with your luggage*—Balance the weight of your luggage on each side, or with one piece of luggage, alternate sides. Use a collapsible, wheeled luggage carrier if possible or use a luggage trolley at the airport.

• *Stop to rest*—You'll probably tire faster during pregnancy. Alternate a day of heavy activity on a trip with one of relaxation, or at least, reduced activity.

• *Get a good night's rest*—A night of good sleep will insure your alertness for the following day's work.

Ten Tips for Getting Enough Sleep on a Business Trip

1. Try to arrange your trip to coincide with your normal sleep time.

2. Allow yourself plenty of time to board your plane or bus so that you can start relaxing immediately. Once you get yourself calm and settled in, you can concentrate on getting some sleep.

3. Motion sickness will definitely interfere with your sleep, so eat lightly before and during your trip.

4. Avoid drinking coffee or eating anything that contains caffeine. Drink decaffeinated tea to help get you sleepy.

5. If the person you're sitting next to is a "talker," politely explain that you need to take a nap and do not wish to be disturbed.

6. Recline your seat as much as possible and lie down on your side. Ask for a pillow to put between your knees to improve circulation or use a small travel bag to keep your feet propped up.

7. Be aware that you may need anywhere from five to twenty minutes to become fully alert after a nap, so don't plan on engaging in any demanding mental activities as soon as you wake up.

8. Try to finish up any pressing project, presentation, or other important work before you attempt to sleep so that your mind is clear and able to rest.

9. Don't be discouraged if falling asleep is difficult the first few times you try. It might take your body time to adjust to the location or time change.

10. Carry a sleep mask with you in case any light keeps you awake. You may also want to bring along some earplugs to keep out unwanted noise, or carry your own radio with headset and relaxing music tape.

Traveling by Car

Your journey to and from work can be the most stressful and tiring part of the day, especially if you have had to stand for long periods.

- *Dress appropriately*—Wear loose, comfortable clothes and flat shoes while traveling.

- *Use a seat belt*—Fasten it loosely over your hips and thighs under the bulge of your abdomen, rather than across it. The shoulder belt should fit snugly between your breasts. If the belt is uncomfortable, relieve the pressure with a piece of folded cloth. Stop driving a car when you can no longer wear a seat belt comfortably or you can no longer fit behind the steering wheel.

- *Adjust the seat*—If you're sitting in the passenger seat, place your seat as far back as possible.

- *Use cruise control*—This feature allows you more freedom to change your position.

- *Stop to stretch*—Long hours of car travel can be very tiring. Stop frequently to stretch, to take a walk, to use the bathroom, get plenty of fluids, or to have a snack.

- *Change your schedule*—Suggest to your boss a change in your working hours so that you're traveling outside rush hour. Perhaps your employer would consider letting you work from your home for one or two days a week.

- *Too much?*—If traveling by car is too much for you, consider starting your maternity leave earlier than you planned.

Traveling by Plane
Most doctors recommend no air travel after the eighth month or thirty-six weeks because of the pressure changes in the cabin. You should also:

- *Check airline regulations*—Travel policies vary with each airline, so ask about restrictions when you book your flight. You may need a note from your doctor.

- *Get plenty of rest beforehand*—Save your energy to cope with problems at the airport, such as long lines, delayed flights, or lost luggage. You can't always count on sleeping on the plane because it's not as easy when you're pregnant.

- *Wear comfortable clothing*—Loose-fitting clothing will help you to relax during a long flight.

• *Eat lightly*—Before and during the flight, keep your food intake low to avoid air sickness.

• *Empty your bladder*—Relieve yourself before the flight. Often the waiting lines are long once you're airborne.

• *Avoid small planes*—Private planes, usually small, have unpressurized cabins. You can also feel the turbulence more than on a larger plane.

• *Ask for an early boarding*—Avoid the crowd by asking for permission to board before the others.

• *Ask for a forward seat*—You'll have a smoother ride if you have a seat in front of the wings. Reserve an aisle seat, which makes it easier to move around and go to the restroom. A bulkhead seat (first row after the division between classes) affords you the opportunity to rest your feet on top of your baggage, but on the negative side, doesn't have luggage storage room.

• *Do exercises to stimulate circulation and relax tense muscles*—Frequent walks up and down the aisle will help prevent swelling and possible blood clots from forming. Stretch your leg, heel first, and gently flex your foot to stretch your calf muscles. Carry a tennis ball in your purse and use it to massage your back. Place the ball between your back and the seat and move your back from side to side. Let the ball drop a little and roll it back and forth again.

• *Stay away from anyone who seems sick*—Ask for a seat change. Try not to touch your tray table or armrest with your hands and wash before eating or touching your face. To be extra safe, wear a face mask to reduce your exposure to germs. Carry a small bottle of antibacterial soap so that you can keep your hands sanitized.

FYI: Exposure to Natural Radiation

Exposure to natural radiation while flying can only increase the risk of miscarriage and/or abnormalities in unborn babies if you are a flight attendant or regular business traveler. That risk is only slightly high for women who only fly a few times a year.

Chapter 2

Ensuring Your Safety at Work

The question of whether working will affect a pregnancy is an important one since more women are in the workplace than ever before. Studies have concluded that babies born to women who worked throughout their pregnancies were just as healthy as those born to women who stayed home. In fact, many doctors believe that the longer you work at a gratifying job, the better it is for your emotional health. You'll discover that staying on the job provides a stability and security when, in other ways, you're going through so many changes.

The length of time you stay on the job depends, of course, on your physical condition and the type of work you do. One benefit that perhaps you hadn't thought about is that the more often pregnant women continue to work until the last minute, the more the pregnant state will be seen by coworkers as perfectly normal. If yours is an uncomplicated pregnancy, you can work at a desk job right up to the start of labor as long as you have a place to rest if it becomes necessary.

Job Safety and the Law

In the past, most pregnant working women found themselves in a no-win job situation. Either they weren't given a choice of whether to work with hazardous chemicals or engage in heavy physical activity, or they were automatically banned from certain jobs by companies that didn't want the women to endanger the health of their fetuses because employers didn't want to risk potential legal liability.

Unfortunately, this corporate attitude has been used historically to deny women equal employment opportunities and to continue to make millions of well-paid industrial jobs off-limits to women. The new laws today are designed to protect pregnant women and new mothers at work. With the advice from your doctor, your employer must make sure that your working conditions won't put your health or your baby's health at risk. That means your employer must do the following:

- Make a risk assessment of any working conditions, processes, or physical, chemical, and biological agents that could jeopardize the health and safety of you or your baby.

- If the assessment reveals a risk, your employer must do all that is reasonable to remove it or prevent your exposure to it.

- If the risk remains, your employer must temporarily alter your working conditions or hours of work.

• If that isn't possible, you must be offered suitable alternative work on terms and conditions that are no less favorable than your original job.

• If there is no suitable alternative work, your employer must suspend you on full pay.

In a nutshell: if you're pregnant, have just given birth, or you're breast-feeding, it's illegal for an employer to dismiss you if you can't do the same job as before due to health and safety risks. If you're in a work situation where you can't always fulfill your job duties because it is too physically stressful, your employer and coworkers are obligated under law to make temporary, common-sense concessions—not gratuitous, embarrassing, or discriminatory ones. (See "Managing Your Maternity Leave," page 106, for more information.)

Identifying Hazards and Dealing with Their Potential Risk

Health experts estimate that as many as twenty million women of child-bearing age work with toxic substances that may damage their ability to give birth to healthy children. Toxins also impair the ability of men to father children, as well as cause birth defects. The National Institute for Occupational Safety and Health (NIOSH) views reproductive disorders as one of the ten most frequent work-related diseases.

The list of hazardous substances and their effects on fetuses is so long and ongoing that it is essential for you to keep abreast of the latest research. Even where the federal government has established safe levels of exposure, as they have for lead, mercury, and other materials, it's worth noting that the thresholds are for adults, not for a developing fetus.

Look under "health effects" on data sheets available to you by your employer. Be vigilant about reading labels on products you use at home and at work. You can look up questionable products on the Internet, and talk with your healthcare provider and your OSHA officer at work about any concerns you have. Handle any suspect materials with care, taking all possible precautions.

If you suspect that you're being exposed to a dangerous substance, ask your employer, employee health department, personnel office, or union representative to specify what it is. By law, you have the right to know, and your employer has the obligation to tell you.

Using Caution with Microwave Ovens

The final word is not in yet about microwave ovens. Experts are not sure whether microwaves are hazardous. They do heat the body though, which may cause reproductive-system damage, cataracts, or may interfere with a pacemaker. In the meantime, you should err on the side of safety and never stand close to one for longer than necessary, especially in the workplace, where these ovens are often placed in small spaces. You can buy a special meter for measuring your oven's electromagnetic field or ask your city department for the service. Follow the manufacturer's instructions to the letter regarding foil and other coverings for the food you're cooking.

How to Avoid Polluted Tap Water

It's true that most municipal water systems deliver safe, potable water to their customers. Other areas, however, have groundwater that has been polluted by chemical seepage from many sources, including factories, toxic dumps, and farms. If you work in such an area, when you turn on the tap you're liable to drink water containing organic chemicals, mutates, or carcinogens. Also, corroded lead pipes, found in many older buildings, are so dangerous that they may cause birth defects.

Whenever there's a question about the water, protect yourself and your baby by doing the following:

- *Check with the local office of the federal Environmental Protection Agency or the local health department about the purity of the water you're drinking—* Notify your employer if the news is bad.

- *Use only bottled water at work and at home—*Or, ask your employer to install a carbon filter on all the faucets in the office.

Staying Away from Harmful Radiation

Two types of radiation are hazardous—ionizing and nonionizing:

- Ionizing is a form of energy capable of changing an atom's structure. Exposure is common in nuclear facilities, health-care institutions, and where foods, spices, cosmetics, and pharmaceuticals are processed with radiation. Although occupational exposure levels are usually low, the danger is from accumulated doses. There is no known safe level of exposure to ionizing radiation. Exposure causes many health problems to women, including cancer, and may cause birth defects in your fetus. Ask to be transferred immediately if you work in such a facility and insist that the new job be at the same level of pay, benefits, and seniority.

• Nonionizing may have adverse health effects, but it does not change the atom's structure. Microwave ovens and other machinery may pose a hazard (see "Using Caution with Microwave Ovens," page 36).

Steering Clear of Cigarette Smoke

Your pregnancy is the best reason yet to stop smoking, if you haven't already done so. Smoking cigarettes is not only bad for you, but can also be hazardous to your baby. Many studies have shown that the dangers include the risk of smaller babies, prematurity, birth defects, and a higher incidence of Sudden Infant Death Syndrome (SIDS). If you need help to stop smoking, ask your doctor for support and medical advice.

Secondhand or passive smoke is equally bad for you. Don't hesitate to ask your partner or your coworkers to smoke someplace where you won't be affected. Here are some tips on how to avoid secondhand smoke:

• Put a sign on your door or on a wall near your workstation asking your coworkers or clients not to smoke near you. Be sure the sign is friendly and simple to avoid alienating anyone.

- Look into buying an ionizer to minimize the effects of smoke that may get into your work space from the hallways, other offices, or the general working area.

Preventing Health Risks from Video-Display Terminals

The experts are not entirely in agreement about the risks of video-display terminals (VDT). Some believe that radiation from VDTs, color TV sets, and other electronic equipment is minimal and may not constitute a danger to pregnant women or fetuses. Others say that women who use computers manufactured from the late 1970s to the mid-1980s, which emit more radiation than new machines, are three-and-a-half times more likely to suffer miscarriages than those whose VDTs emit low-level fields. If your equipment at work is this old, speak to your employer about upgrading, and take these precautions:

1. *Test the terminal*—VDTs are supposed to have lead shielding to avoid radiation hazards, but a simple (yet expensive) test can be purchased from most electronic stores and used to be sure yours has no emissions. If it does, ask your employer to replace your current monitor with a lower-emission model. Note that computers with liquid-crystal display, gas plasma, or electroluminescent screens do not emit significant radiation.

2. *Reduce use*—Cut down on the time you spend in front of the monitor, if possible, and turn it off when not in use.

3. *Increase distance*—Radiation reduces dramatically with distance, so keep a full arm's length (approximately twenty-eight inches) away from the monitor. Use a detachable keyboard. Because radiation fields are more intense from the sides and back, try to stay four to five feet away from your coworkers' terminals.

4. *Use a mesh filter*—You can buy a mesh filter from your local computer store that fits over a computer screen to reduce glare and prevent the formation of an electromagnetic field. The filters absorb radiation from the screen and safely drain it away, although that doesn't reduce the risk from the sides, bottom, and top of the machine.

Watch out for Signs of Carpal Tunnel Syndrome (CTS)

Twenty-eight percent of all pregnant women experience Carpal Tunnel Syndrome. The extra fluid in the body can cause swollen feet, hands, and legs; in hands and wrists, this extra fluid can compress the median nerve, producing CTS. If your job involves repetitive hand and wrist movement, be on the lookout for any pain, numbness, or tingling of the hands and wrists.

Try to restrict repetitive physical activity or find ways to accomplish tasks with less bending of the wrists. Wear a splint on one or both wrists or put pillows under your affected wrist during sleep. Kneel on hands and knees, lean your body forward stretching your wrists, hold for a few seconds. Hold your hand above your head and wiggle your fingers. Keep the working environment warm and dry. Fifty milligrams per day of vitamin B-6 can also help your muscles to stay pain-free.

Redesign Your Workstation

The largest number of VDT-related ailments result from repetitive keystrokes at poorly designed workstations. Finding solutions to the ergonomic needs of the human body and poor station design can reduce the muscle fatigue, eyestrain, and repetitive trauma injuries that plague VDT operators. Try adjusting your chair so that the back of the chair supports the small of your back. A spring-loaded chair is best. Otherwise, use a chiropractic cushion and a footrest.

Ensuring Auto Safety

Statistics tell us that the greatest danger of accidents anyone faces is going to and coming from work behind the wheel of a car. Be extra cautious while driving and don't take chances! Here are six effective tips for auto safety:

1. Plan your route ahead of time if you're going to an unfamiliar place for a meeting or other work-related activity.

2. Always wear your seat belt, even if it causes some discomfort. (They are required by law in all states.)

3. Drive slowly, even if you're used to traveling at moderately high speeds.

4. Avoid night driving, if possible.

5. Always keep easy-to-follow maps in the car or use a GPS navigational system to help you find your way if your car has one.

6. Keep a supply of plastic bags, mints, crackers, cell phone or change for a phone call, and bottled water in the car in case you feel sick while you're driving. If this happens, pull over to the side of the road or get off at the next exit.

JOB SAFETY CHECKLIST

In order to analyze exactly what hazards you may be facing at work, fill out the following checklist and take it to your next checkup. Your physician should be up to date on the newest research results about these possible dangers and how they may affect you. If you work in an industrial facility, be sure you see a company nurse or doctor as soon as you learn that you're pregnant.

Number of hours you work per week including overtime: _____

Total amount of time per week that you stand: _____

Total amount of time each day for breaks and lunch: _____

Average daily temperature in office: _____

Commuting hours per week: _____

Pressure from deadlines or work load   Yes   No
Describe: _____
_____

Exposure to cigarette smoke   Yes   No
Describe: _____
_____

Mental and physical fatigue and other physical burdens   Yes   No

Describe: _____

_____

_____

Strenuous movements and postures   Yes   No

Describe: _____

_____

_____

Exposure to loud noises   Yes   No

Describe: _____

_____

_____

Exposure to extreme hot or cold   Yes   No

Describe: _____

_____

_____

Exposure to shocks, vibration, or movement   Yes   No

Describe: _____

_____

_____

Exposure to poor quality air   Yes   No

Describe: _____

_____

_____

Exposure to biological and chemical agents, mercury and mercury derivatives, lead and lead derivatives, gases, carbon monoxide, or toxins   Yes   No

Describe: _____

_____

_____

Exposure to other hazards   Yes   No

Describe: _____

_____

_____

Preventing Late-Term Risks

As you near the end of your term, there may be some risks involved in physically carrying out your job duties. Be aware of the possible risks involved in doing the following routine activities:

Standing

Throughout your pregnancy, shift your weight often when you're standing for long periods in order to lessen the strain on your back muscles. Wear thick, rubber-soled shoes when you're standing on hard surfaces, such as concrete. Studies show that standing for many hours at work after the twenty-eighth week may cause your blood pressure to rise and your baby's weight to be somewhat lower than average. The risk increases with each additional week.

If your job requires standing more than four hours a day, the American Medical Association recommends that you stop working by the twenty-fourth week unless you can sit for thirty minutes out of every hour. In that case, they recommend you leave by the thirty-second week. The discomforts of standing for long periods during the last few weeks may include backache, varicose veins, and hemorrhoids.

Strenuous or Stressful Activity

It's been noted in recent studies that strenuous or physically stressful activity during the last half of pregnancy may result in smaller than average babies and in damage to the areas of the placenta. For example, women who stand for more than four hours at a job without a break have a higher risk of preterm labor.

Since pregnancy puts a considerable demand upon your emotional and physical state, it is important for you to try to eliminate, if possible, anything that could potentially impact your body negatively. So if your job is just generally stressful, cutting back on work or getting solid rest is all you may need. At the moment, it's believed that these factors will not lead to any long-term physical or mental problems in your baby, but research continues.

Lifting, Climbing, or Bending

If you have a job that requires an intensive amount of lifting, climbing, or bending, experts recommend that you leave after the twentieth week, or after the twenty-eighth week if the activity is moderate. Until then, always squat, face the object, and lift it with a straight back. Hold the object close to your chest when you straighten your legs.

Shift Work

Shift work can have a significant impact on health. It may disrupt sleep and cause mood and digestive imbalances. Studies have shown that workers on rotating shifts do better when they're about to take a few days off before changing to a different shift. If your work involves night shifts, you have the right to transfer to suitable alternative day work or, if none is available, to be suspended on full pay.

You must tell your employer in writing that you are pregnant and provide them with a medical certificate from your doctor or midwife stating that you cannot work at night for health and safety reasons. If you do this, your employer must transfer you.

Potential Modifications

If you are worried about health and safety at work, discuss your concerns with your doctor or midwife and ask for a letter stating that the working conditions are harmful to you and/or your baby. The following actions can be considered when modifying your job:

- Restricted to lifting up to twenty-five pounds

- Assigned less physical tasks

- Adjusted work hours (e.g., flexible scheduling, day shift rather than night)

- Varied tasks to avoid static posture

- Limited standing time to less than three hours a day

- Modified break schedule (e.g., shorter, more frequent breaks)

- Reduced amount of work performed at heights (such as on ladders or stepstools)

- Installed footrests (for seated and standing workers) so that one foot can be alternately raised

- Adjusted height of work surfaces and chairs

The following organizations will provide you with safety guidelines or carry out a risk assessment for you so that you can take action against your employer. You may also be able to claim compensation in an employment tribunal:

- *NIOSH*—The National Institute for Occupational Safety and Health has consultants who answer specific questions about workplace toxins and stresses.

- *OSHA*—Write to the Occupational Safety and Health Administration. In order to obtain the best service, identify specific hazards that concern you.

- *Manufacturers*—Write directly to the manufacturer's corporate medical director to learn about the safety of equipment you use at work.

- *National Association of Working Women*—Call their Job Problem Hotline at (800) 522-0925.

- *Safety representative, local Health and Safety executive, or Environmental Health Department*—Check your phone book.

- *Unions*—Contact your local union or the Coalition of Labor Union Women for the booklet on workplace hazards, "Is Your Job Making You Sick?"

Chapter 3

Keeping Fit at Work

Exercising during pregnancy will raise your energy level, give you strength and flexibility, promote deep and restful sleep, and often help to curb depression. If you exercise during your pregnancy, it will be easier for you to get back into shape after your baby is born.

Think of exercise as an opportunity to spend a little time on yourself to relax, to soothe tensions and anxieties, and to alleviate common discomforts of pregnancy, such as backache, varicose veins, cramps, and constipation.

Exercising on the Go

A good exercise program can easily be built right into your busy lifestyle. For example:

- *Walk to work*—Skip a ride in good weather and walk to work. Or park your car or leave a bus some distance from work and walk the remaining distance. Take a yoga class or go swimming before or after work.

- *Turn every action into exercise*—For example, whenever you drop something, make it an opportunity to squat and exercise your thigh muscles. As you squat, contract your pelvic muscles. Also, get from one office to another by using the stairs instead of the elevator.

- *Use daily chores*—When you're replenishing office supplies or rearranging your workspace, stretch farther than necessary to work your muscles harder.

- *Buy exercise equipment*—Try expandable latex exercise bands. They're small enough to take anywhere. Do a few stretches on your break or while talking on the phone.

- *Be flexible*—Find a variety of activities you enjoy so you can fit some form of exercise into every day.

A Word of Caution

The American College of Obstetricians and Gynecologists currently recommends the following:

- Consult your physician for guidelines before beginning any exercise program, particularly if you have diabetes, a heart or respiratory condition, high blood pressure, or high cholesterol.

- Exercise should never be undertaken if you have medical conditions, such as *diastasis recti* (separation of the rectus abdominis muscle) or *placenta previa* (the placenta is implanted completely over or near the cervix).

- Do not attempt any exercise if your doctor has ordered you to bed.

- After the first trimester, pregnant women should avoid supine (on your back) positions during exercise.

- Exercise guidelines differ from physician to physician and from woman to woman, so use good common sense, consult your doctor, and adapt to your changing body.

Prenatal Workout

To make exercising at work as easy as possible, keep the proper clothing handy, such as:

- Loose-fitting garments or stretch wear that breathes.

- Good support bras, such as a sports bra, found in most large sportswear and department stores. Wear a maternity bra under a sports bra for super support.

- Very good aerobic shoes for protection against injury, or lightweight walking shoes with substantial heel cushioning and flexible soles.

Walking shoes should feel comfortable, but not too cushiony. Buy them in a sporting goods store where trained personnel can help you. Always wear socks—never nylons—when you walk and wear support hose if you have circulation problems. Cotton socks absorb perspiration, which might otherwise damage your shoes or cause blisters.

Now Begin Exercising

These exercises are meant to maintain, or improve, your general muscle tone and flexibility. Special emphasis is placed on exercises to strengthen your pelvic floor and abdominal muscles. Your comfort and safety will be determined largely by your state of health and fitness before you were pregnant.

Most of these exercises have been designed to be done at your work place either while sitting or standing. It's even better if you have access to a private area that's carpeted or cushioned. Play appropriate music on a headset to make the session more rhythmic and enjoyable.

Each exercise mentions a recommended number of repetitions, but do the work at your own slower or faster pace. In all cases, however, start with two or three repetitions and work up to more.

Easy Warm-up Exercises

Don't neglect this even when you're rushed. Your joints are more susceptible to injury now because of the relaxing effect of hormones on your connective tissues. These exercises will also maintain adequate circulation and ensure mobility of your joints, especially your legs.

• *Deep breaths*—Standing with legs comfortably apart, knees slightly bent, slowly reach arms toward the ceiling, lifting rib cage and spine as you inhale deeply. Slowly lower arms while exhaling. Repeat three to five times.

• *Neck*—Slowly touch chin to chest four times. Then slowly rotate head in a circle to release tension and to relax shoulders. Reverse the direction of rotation.

• *Shoulders*—Gently lift one shoulder up to ear and hold. Then press shoulder down as far as possible to relieve tension buildup. Repeat with other shoulder. Repeat eight times on each side. Then circle shoulders backward four times, forward four times, and backward four times to loosen chest muscles. (Try not to hold the phone receiver between your shoulder and ear while you talk or reach for things; it's a sure way to end up with added neck and shoulder pains.)

• *Arms*—Relax shoulders and drop arms to sides. Inhale deeply, raise one arm high over head, stretching from the waist. Wiggle fingers and exhale as you slowly lower arm. Repeat several times with each arm. End by vigorously shaking both hands.

• *Lower body*—Standing with legs apart in line with shoulders, gently lunge side to side being careful that knees don't press farther forward than toes. Repeat eight times.

- *Ankles and feet*—Sit on a chair, preferably a straight-backed one, for comfort and support. Lift one foot slightly off the floor. Make smooth circles at the ankles, first in one direction and then the other. Pump one foot or both feet up and down vigorously thirty times. Do this several times a day. Don't ever cross your legs.

- *Your entire body*—Start by slowly marching in place while lifting your legs and arms up high. Continue marching for a couple minutes.

Simple Stretching Exercises

When you're doing these exercises, stretch just to the point of mild, comfortable tension, never pain. Hold stretches for ten to thirty seconds.

- *Upper back*—While sitting or standing, hold arms out to the side even with shoulders, palms forward. Cross arms over chest with palms touching rib cage. "Walk" fingers around back, drop chin to chest, and curl slightly forward. Hold. Feel the stretch between shoulder blades and the base of the neck.

- *Chest and biceps*—Seated or standing, clasp hands behind body and lift slightly. Don't bend forward; keep back long and straight. Hold. Feel the stretch in chest and upper arms.

- *Triceps (back of arms)*—Place palm of one hand on the same side shoulder. Now raise elbow, sliding palm to back between shoulder blades, elbows facing ceiling. Grasp elbow with the other hand and pull behind head until stretch is felt. Hold. Repeat with other arm.

- *Torso*—Place one hand on hip and curve other arm over head. Bend body sideways, stretching overhead arm. Repeat on the other side. This helps relieve pressure under ribs and shortness of breath, both of which are common in the last trimester.

- *Spine*—Stand with legs shoulder-width apart and hands on thighs supporting body weight. Slowly round back, tucking tailbone under, until back is shaped like a C. Gently roll back to starting position. Repeat twice.

- *Quadriceps (front of thigh)*—In standing position, hold onto a chair with one hand and reach the other hand behind your body, bend knee and left opposite foot backward so that you can grasp ankle, and touch buttock with heel. Straighten body with knees together. Hold. If the muscle is too tight, hold on to your sock or pant leg until you can reach ankle.

- *Hamstrings*—Stand with right foot forward and heel pressed to the floor. With weight on the left foot, bend right knee. Repeat with other leg.

- *Calves*—Facing a wall, place right foot forward and bend right knee. Keep left foot stretched behind. Lean against wall, pressing left foot into the floor and right knee forward. Repeat with other leg. Do two times for each leg.

Aerobic Exercise

The easiest and most convenient exercise during the workday is simply to take a walk, alone or with a coworker.

Start out slowly and steadily build up to a mile at a brisk, comfortable pace. Inhale deeply, making sure both your abdomen and chest expand. Take several short walks if one long one tires you. Keep your chin up and body relaxed. Walk with an even, natural stride. Let your arms swing at your sides; weights on your arms or legs will only add stress to already unstable joints. Walk only where there's sure footing and don't overexert yourself. Slow down when you're nearing the end. This is an excellent way to tone muscles, fill lungs with fresh air, stay regular, and sleep well at night. Your stamina and energy will increase and fatigue will decrease. In bad weather, at your office, lift legs two and a half inches from the floor and walk in place, fifty-five paces a minute.

Body-Strengthening Exercises

• *Shoulders and chest*—Stand or sit with your arms held out in front of you at shoulder level, elbows bent. Squeeze elbows together, tightening chest muscles at the same time. Repeat twelve times.

• *Arms*—Do wall push-ups when you have a minute or two by placing your hands at chest level with your feet several inches behind your body. Lean forward toward the wall, and then slowly push back.

• *Legs, hips, buttocks, and thighs*—Stand to the side of a chair back or against a wall supporting yourself with right hand. Slowly raise left leg forward with knee turned outward as high as you can without swinging. Pause, then lower leg. Shake out. Extend left leg to front, then down. Then lift to the side, and back down. Then lean forward lightly with right knee bent and with left leg pointing to the back. Lift left heel toward the ceiling, then lower to the floor. Repeat four positions with the other leg, always exhaling on the extension. Do each exercise twelve times for each leg. Afterward, contract buttocks muscles while standing, holding tightly for count of two and releasing to a count of two.

• *Pelvic, abdominal, and back muscles*—The pelvic floor consists of a group of muscles that support the pelvic organs. It's important that they be exercised regularly; not only will they help with your delivery, they will also correct your posture, relieve backaches, and help your muscles to regain strength quickly after birth. Strong muscles will relieve stress incontinence and make sex more satisfying.

These pelvic exercises, known more commonly as Kegels, can be done in any position, anywhere, and without anyone being aware. Start doing them three times a day and work your way up to twenty. To begin with, tighten vaginal and pelvic muscles as though holding back urine (without tensing abdominal, thigh, and buttock muscles), hold for a count of five, and relax. Repeat five times. You can test your muscles by actually attempting to stop the flow of urine in midstream.

To practice a seated pelvic tilt, sit on the edge of a chair, knees apart with hands resting on them. Rock backward, drawing abdominal muscles in firmly, and rounding the back. Then gently rock forward, releasing abdominal muscles, and returning your back to its natural curvature. Do this slowly, counting to twelve as you tighten the muscles, or do it quickly to loosen a stiff back after sitting for a long time.

To practice a standing pelvic tilt, keep arms by your side and feet slightly apart. Stand against a wall to help you get the movement right. Relax shoulders, breathe normally. Tilt your pelvis backward and forward, drawing stomach muscles in and your bottom under, allowing back to arch slightly. Hold for five seconds, relax, and inhale. Do this twelve times.

Do this breathing exercise at your desk. Breathe deeply and expand abdominal muscles. Hold for a second and exhale slowly as you contract stomach muscles. Do this five or six times each chance you get.

Postpartum Exercise

Even the busiest working mom can find ten minutes a day to do a few exercises, climb stairs, or walk a couple of blocks. That means that the sooner you start an exercise program, the sooner the pounds will melt away.

You'll find that tensions of the job are noticeably reduced, even after the first exercise session, and that the benefits last for several hours. When you have a knotty problem to solve, summon up mental energies by working up a good sweat through exercise.

In addition to exercising, standing and sitting properly will do wonders to improve your appearance. A good posture can take five inches off your waist. After months of having to adapt to an expanding abdomen, your body needs to be reminded of its normal upright position. Don't slump in your chair or walk with rounded shoulders, sagging breasts, and loose tummy. Walk tall and sit way back in a chair with a cushion behind your waist and your chest lifted.

Postpartum Exercise Guidelines

Your doctor will tell you when to begin. Most new moms should wait at least six weeks before starting any impact exercises, such as jogging. In the case of a Caesarean, your doctor will probably advise a six-to-ten week wait. You're usually given guidelines for doing the proper exercises at certain points in your recovery.

Use the exercises on pages 54–55 to warm up and stretch. Continue with your prenatal exercise, such as the pelvic tilt, and then slowly add the exercises below to your program as you increase your strength and endurance. Finally, add aerobic exercises (page 57) and work up to a sustained thirty to forty-five minute at least three times a week.

Now Begin Exercising

- *Kegels*—These exercises are a crucial part of your recovery. If you fail to tighten your stretched pelvic muscles, you could be subject to urinary incontinence (leaking urine when you cough, laugh, or sneeze) or reduced sensations during sexual intercourse.

- *Abdominal muscles*—While sitting or standing, contract your abdominal muscles and hold for five seconds while you continue breathing naturally. As you become more proficient, increase the contraction to ten seconds. (After a Caesarean, you might have trouble feeling your abdominal muscles working. In that case, place your hand on your belly to follow the action better.)

- *Hips, thighs, and bottom*—Tone your legs and bottom with leg lifts when you're on the phone or any time you're standing for a few moments. In a standing position, lift one leg with knee bent up toward your body, and return your foot to the floor. To tone hip and thigh, raise your leg from your side up twelve to fourteen inches, and return to the starting position. To tone your buttocks, lift one leg toward your back with the knee slightly bent, and slowly return your foot to the floor.

- *Back and arms*—Stretch your entire back and shoulders by standing with your back against a wall, hands at your sides and heels, hips, and shoulders pressed against the wall. Slowly raise your arms over your head, keeping your hands and elbows touching the wall.

- *Climb stairs*—Stair climbing, especially at work, will burn ten times more calories a minute than standing in an elevator. It will also tone leg and buttock muscles and strengthen the heart.

- *Vary activities*—Go to a lunchtime yoga class one day and go swimming before work the next. Don't allow boredom to undermine your exercising.

- *Use accessories*—Leg and arm exercises are more effective if you use workout rubber bands. Small hand weights (or substitute with soup cans) are good for upper-body strength development.

- *Start walking*—Walk half a mile in seventeen minutes three times a week. After a couple of weeks, increase it to a mile in thirty-two minutes four or five times a week. Gradually reduce the time to twenty minutes. Your eventual goal should be to walk up to three miles at a fifteen-minute-a-mile pace. A pedometer from a sporting goods store will clock the miles.

- *Exercise with your baby*—Pick up your baby after work and go to a Mommy and Me exercise class or see "Five Exercises You Can Do with Your Baby" outlined in the next section.

Exercises You Can Do with Your Baby
Exercising with your baby after work combines cuddling time with the workout you need.

- *Abdominal muscles and lower back*—Lie back, knees bent, feet on floor. Place your baby on your hips in a sitting position, squeeze buttocks together and raise hips, then release. Do two sets of twenty.

- Lie on back, left leg bent, right ankle crossed over left knee. Place baby on your belly using right hand for support. Reach left hand over right knee. Release back down. Do eight to ten times on one side, and then repeat on other side. Do two sets.

- Lie on back with knees bent, pelvis tilted up. Hold baby on your belly with one hand and put other hand behind your head. Lift upper body and curl toward the baby, then relax. Do two sets of ten.

- *Chest and biceps*—Lying on your back with knees bent, lift your baby toward the ceiling and back down. Do two sets of ten.

- *Arms*—Standing with feet comfortably apart and knees slightly bent, hold baby close to your belly, then slowly lift to chest, drawing elbows up to but not higher than shoulders. Lower baby and lift again. Do two sets eight to twelve times.

Chapter 4

On-the-Job Stress Reducers and Relaxation Techniques

Stress is a normal part of life, but working women seem to have more than their share. As a pregnant working woman, you need to be sure that the stress in your life doesn't adversely affect your health and the health of your baby. If you can't fight or flee, learn how to flow.

Ten Ways to Control Stress at Work

Have you had trouble sleeping lately? Suffer from headaches, stomachaches, or heartburn? Or do you seem to develop one cold after another? Perhaps that's your body's way of reacting to too much stress. Here are some general strategies for reducing the impact:

1. *Organize your workload*—Tasks are more manageable if you deal with them one at a time. When you have too many things to do at work, draw up a plan of attack in order of priority. Complete the tasks one after the other and soon you'll find the weight lifting from your shoulders.

2. *Solve the problems*—Begin by identifying the true problems. If you're always overwhelmed at the office, think about why you tend to take on so much. Devise several ways to solve the problem and write them down. Put your plan into action and evaluate it to see if it's working.

3. *Avoid the source of stress*—Don't make major changes in your life until after your baby is born. Beware of the holiday season; let someone else do the work this year. Clean up the clutter on your desk. Give up stressful volunteer tasks.

4. *Return stress to its rightful owner*—Some of the aggravation you feel is really someone else's problem. Tell your mate that he'll have to entertain his clients himself; tell a coworker to learn the system instead of always asking you. Start saying no to the other people who lean on you. Explain that you have more than enough to do, and suggest that they should do it themselves.

5. *Try physical activity*—Exercise, yoga, or perhaps a stroll around your workplace during the day is a wonderful stress reliever. Even cleaning your work space in your first trimester can relax you.

6. *Talk about it*—Share your concerns with a coworker or a friend. It may or may not lead to a solution, but you'll feel much better after unburdening yourself. If sharing with a friend doesn't seem to help, be sensible and seek the counsel of a professional.

7. *Don't hold back the tears*—Crying is a healthy way to relieve anxiety. Of course, there are times when it wouldn't be appropriate: in front of a client, for instance.

8. *Accept differences and things you cannot change*—Some problems simply cannot be solved or else the solution is way down the road. Don't let it bother you if coworkers do things differently from the way you do. Relax, there's more than one way to reach a goal. Cooperation is always better than confrontation.

9. *Keep up a social life*—Visit friends, take a colleague to a play, go out to dinner with another couple. Make time for fun. Allow time in your busy week for your favorite recreation and watch how the tension disappears.

10. *Get plenty of sleep and rest*—See "Sleeping Well and Working Refreshed," page 23. Be sure to eat well too. Stress seems to deplete B vitamins so quickly that it causes a pregnant woman to become deficient in this group of vitamins.

A word to the wise: Drugs and alcohol are temporary anxiety relievers—they will not permanently remove the sources of stress. That doesn't take into consideration what these substances may do to you and your baby. Never drink alcohol or take medication without a doctor's consent or prescription.

On-the-Job Relaxation Techniques

The relaxation techniques that you learn now will serve you all your life. Try each method a few times to find out which works best for you. Then practice relaxation for ten minutes, twice a day. Most people find that it takes a couple of weeks to become proficient. Once you've learned the techniques, you'll be able to do them in the middle of a crowd.

Regular use of these techniques will make you more serene and more capable of dealing with the stress of work and pregnancy. These exercises will also help you to focus your attention inward. Your body will receive the message that you're safe and secure. Your muscles will relax, your pulse rate will drop, and you'll find your anxiety has decreased. Before you begin practicing, make sure conditions are right:

- *Privacy*—It's best if you can avoid being disturbed. Pick a quiet place and close the door. Take the phone off the hook, if possible.

- *Comfort*—Sit in a comfortable chair, take your shoes off, loosen your clothing, and close your eyes.

- *Concentration*—Don't allow anything to distract you. If your thoughts wander, refocus your attention on the technique.

- *Duration*—Make sure you practice at least ten minutes every day. Take the time during the workday even if you're very busy. Once you've relaxed, you'll find your efficiency will improve, making up for lost time.

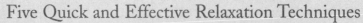

Five Quick and Effective Relaxation Techniques

1. Deep breathing—Slowly breathe in for a count of seven and exhale through pursed lips for seven counts. The exhalation should be like an audible sigh of relief. To be sure the exhalation is complete, count to yourself one thousand and one, one thousand and two—up to seven counts. Keep the breath light and soft and high in your throat.

2. Muscle relaxation—This method, which can be easily done at your desk, involves releasing tension in different parts of your body in sequence. Choose a particular muscle, then tense and release until you feel in control of that muscle. Do this with one muscle after another. If one resists, pull it into the position of relaxation; for instance, drop your tight jaw and hold it in that position until your face relaxes. This technique is especially useful if you tend to carry a lot of tension in your forehead or shoulders. This skill will also serve you well during labor when your uterus will contract involuntarily while you will be able to relax the rest of your body.

3. Meditation—You've relaxed your body; now it's time for your mind. Concentrate all your attention on the exercise you're doing. Deeply relax all your muscles. Breathe normally through your nose. Repeat a single word or a phrase to yourself over and over: this is called a mantra. Chant the word in rhythm with your breathing. Prevent troubling thoughts from entering your consciousness. If they do, refocus. When you're in a deeply relaxed meditative state, your blood pressure and heart rate drop, which enhances your feeling of well-being.

4. Mindfulness—Like meditation, this technique encourages moment-to-moment awareness. Focus on the present only or the job you are doing rather than letting your mind wander to what needs to be done or other worries.

5. Guided imagery—Close your eyes and look within. Picture yourself in a relaxing situation. For example, imagine you're gliding in a canoe over the quiet blue waters of a mountain lake. Listen to the slap of the water on the boat, the sound of a bird singing, and feel the warmth of the sun. Studies have shown that blue is a particularly relaxing color for your imagined scene.

Fast-Acting Stress Busters

- *Thought Stoppers*—If you're worried about the meeting tomorrow or how you'll be able to pay for future day care, slowly pass the word "stop" through your mind. Replay the letters S-T-O-P over and over. Or count backward from five to zero. Imagine each letter or number in vivid color.

- *Worry Time*—When you start to stress about something, set it aside in your mind (or write it down) and then go back to your work. Set aside a few minutes every day to deal with your worries in a more productive way.

- *Aromatherapy*—Use highly concentrated oils from plants and herbs to relax, recharge, and increase your sense of well-being. They are also good for dealing with environmental stress caused by loud noises and bright lights; physical stress from repetitive-strain syndrome, muscular fatigue, and backaches; mental stress created by financial and job concerns; and chemical stress caused by consuming too much junk food and coffee, or breathing polluted air in your office or factory. You can purchase essential oils in health, beauty, herb, and natural-food stores. Use these oils in your place of employment simply by placing a few drops of oil on your wrist or earlobe, in small humidifiers, light bulbs, spray atomizer, room diffusers, or in water bowls.

Note: If you share space, the aroma sensitivity of your coworkers should be taken into consideration. Although these fragrant oils don't have FDA approval as medication, aromatherapy proponents say that they will aid various health concerns. While most essential oils are nontoxic, to stay on the safe side, check with your doctor or the American Aromatherapy Association first.

Chapter 5

Maintaining Your Professional Appearance

Good grooming and good taste never change. You'll want to maintain the same professional image even while your silhouette is noticeably expanding. When you look for maternity clothes, look for appropriate styles that not only reflect your professional attitude, but also make you feel great.

Guidelines for Buying Maternity Clothes

Nowadays, designers are offering smarter styles and better fabric choices to mothers-to-be. If you love (or have) to wear two-piece suits to work, there are many fabulous and affordable options. If you weren't comfortable wearing hosiery prepregnancy, you don't have to start wearing them now.

There are many new styles in maternity pants and pant suits to select from, ranging from basic leggings, to boot legs, to flair bottoms. While basic black is always a secure choice, the newest shades like soft lilac and

French blue are wonderful as well. Shop carefully for coordinated items and you'll have a varied wardrobe for work that is not only comfortable but practical as well.

When to Shop

Many pregnant women are in their fourth or fifth month before their regular clothes begin to feel tight. Others find their waistbands getting snug at the beginning of the fourth month. Some women feel it in their waist and breasts; others just expand in general. Rather than buying your whole maternity wardrobe all at once, shop in stages—at three months, at five months—and then add items from time to time to keep you feeling fresh and well dressed.

Where to Shop

Your choices include discount department stores (like Wal-Mart and K-Mart), specialty boutiques, online companies, and mail-order houses geared to pregnant working women, offering a wide variety to choose from. Since most department stores have closed their maternity sections, in many cities there are stores specializing in fashionable work and play maternity apparel. Often, they're situated in a business section so that you can shop on your lunch hour with a coworker.

But don't despair if your city doesn't have any maternity boutiques. Mail-order catalogs carry a large selection of imaginative and classic business maternity clothes. You'll find them listed in most women's magazines. Many of these mail-order houses have personal shoppers to help you choose over the phone.

Essential Buying Tips

Keep your maternity wardrobe simple and businesslike. The National Association of Female Executives has done research showing that the less businesslike a woman looks, the less competent she's perceived to be—particularly if she's pregnant.

1. *Purchase separates in solid, neutral colors*—Navy, brown, gray, camel, with small, subtle patterns. Add some interest with texture in the material such as ribbing. Remember that dark colors will deemphasize your shape more than light colors will. If color is acceptable in your work environment, venture from black to contemporary burgundies and eggplants.

2. *Concentrate on quality, not quantity*—A few good outfits beat many more thrown-together ones. Two or three skirts, some jumpers and pants, and four or five coordinated tops should be enough for work, especially when you vary the accessories. Some of these can be worn even after your baby is born.

3. *Ask about return policies before your purchase*—Many stores will allow you to make an exchange or receive store credit. If so, make sure to try the clothes on. Many mail-order and Internet maternity boutiques will permit returns because of your inability to try on selections, but be aware of time restrictions and calculate the cost of return or exchange shipping in your decision to buy.

4. *Draw attention away from your middle by wearing stylish jewelry and colorful scarves at the neckline*—Avoid wide or shiny belts, chunky bracelets, hip ruffles, or gathers at the waist. One-color ensembles emphasize a long, lean look. Stretch cotton materials are comfortable, but avoid clingy materials

that reveal every bulge. Add height to a round face by wearing your hair pulled back from your face. To attract attention away from your body, accentuate your best facial feature—beautiful eyes, a generous mouth.

5. *Be sure your clothing fits properly before you buy it*—There should be ample room for expansion in the bust line, and clothing should be designed with adjustable straps and buttons and elastic tape at the waist and under the belly. Maternity clothes come in regular women's sizes. For example, a size twelve maternity dress is designed to fit a size twelve woman with an expanded waistline. If you have gained a large amount of weight in general, you'll have to buy accordingly. You don't have to guess what something will look like later in your pregnancy—maternity shops have three-month and five-month pillows to use as guides. Avoid garments that have a tight waistline or belt, or that fit closely around the thighs and in the crotch.

6. *Be practical*—Avoid impulsive shopping sprees. Start slowly and work your way up, selecting clothes that will work well together. Remember that you may continue to wear maternity clothes after the birth, until your body gets back into shape. So if you're planning to breast-feed, choose styles that will be practical for feeding—tops or dresses that undo or are easy to pull up. (See the following section.)

Choosing Tops

- Buy lightweight blouses because of the tendency to overheat during pregnancy. Try not to wear anything too clingy.

- Tops come in trapeze shapes, A-line cuts, and tunic length. Vests add slimming, vertical lines to an outfit. Empire-waist styles are flattering since they have a high waistline and show off your curves.

- Wear shirts with a collar that will accentuate your collarbones, like a scoop neck, boat, or V-neck. These, paired with a blazer, will make your neck appear long and lean.

- Wear your fitted jackets as long as you can; simply unbutton the bottom buttons for extra room. Unbutton more as you grow, until you're finally forced to keep it open. Or toss on a light shirt/jacket over a more fitted top/pant for a little extra coverage. Later, buy a maternity blazer.

Choosing Maternity Bras

During pregnancy and breast-feeding, your bra size will probably change two or three times. The typical woman will gain an extra two inches under the bust and two inches across the bust during pregnancy, while her breasts can become a pound and a half heavier, putting a strain on the supporting, nonelastic tissues. If you don't lift some of the weight from these ligaments, they will stretch and your breasts will sag permanently.

Most women find their regular bras too uncomfortable beyond the fourth or fifth month of pregnancy and switch to maternity bras. Keep these points in mind when you're selecting maternity bras:

- Measurements should be taken directly under your breasts for correct size and around the fullest part for cup size. Check the overall fit of the bra: if it's riding up at the back, it's too small. It's best to be fitted by a trained bra fitter (available in most maternity and lingerie shops).

- Buy at least two bras that feel as comfortable as your skin. You'll probably be wearing them day and night for several months.

- Always try on a bra before buying. A high cotton content will keep you cool. Look for well-finished inside seams. Don't buy a plastic-lined bra; it can cause soreness, cracking, and infections.

- Wide, non-stretch straps (that won't cut into your shoulders) will help to spread the weight and prevent sagging. Three or four hooks will provide better support. To hold your breasts securely, get an uplift or sling-type bra that raises your breasts upward and inward. Stay away from bras that flatten your breasts.

- Look for soft styling without underwiring, which may press against the delicate breast tissue.

• For a nursing bra, check whether you can manage the flap on the cup with one hand (you'll be holding your baby with the other). If the cup unhooks from the shoulder strap, your breast will be unsupported during nursing. Also, the loose strap is likely to fall off your shoulder, requiring two hands to close it. Both the flap-opening and front-opening types give good support during and after breast feeding.

Choosing a Girdle/Maternity Belt

The primary purpose of a maternity girdle is to support your uterus from below without compressing it. The girdle also supports your back and relieves muscle strain, which is especially helpful when you've already had children. A knowledgeable salesperson will fit you with an expanding-panel girdle, not a reinforcing one. Some find maternity girdles unnecessary and uncomfortable, particularly in warm weather.

There are also special maternity belts that fit around your lower back and under your belly to cradle the often uncomfortable baby weight that can cause back strain, abdominal discomfort, or sciatic pain toward the end of your pregnancy. Originally designed to be worn discretely under your clothing, some maternity-wear makers offer maternity belts in bold colors and bright patterns. Wear them on the outside, particularly over a leotard or yoga clothing, to provide support during exercise.

Choosing Panties

Some women wear regular briefs or bikini panties or light cotton thongs in a larger size during pregnancy; others wear full-size maternity underpants or special maternity thongs. Fabric is your main consideration. Wear panties that are comfortable, soft, breathable, and hold up in the washer. Pima cotton is especially soft and comfortable, although a little pricey. Elastic should be wide and soft, and seams should be minimal—some cotton knit panties now have completely seamless sides.

Choosing Hosiery

During pregnancy, the circulation in your legs is apt to be sluggish; therefore, it's important that if you wear pantyhose, wear it with a nonrestricting waistband and roomy toes. Maternity support pantyhose, which adapts to your movements and permits free circulation, is helpful if you spend a lot of time on your feet at work. Some women are perfectly happy with queen-size pantyhose, however.

Avoid knee-high stockings and socks with tight, elastic tops, which can restrict your blood flow. Create a slimming monochromatic line with stockings that match your skirt. If you're experiencing varicose veins, opt for opaque tights, but otherwise show some skin.

Saving Money on Your Maternity Wardrobe

You'll only need maternity wear for a few months, so why spend hundreds of dollars when you could save the money for something more important? Unfortunately, the IRS does not allow a business deduction for maternity clothes even if your company insists on certain clothes for work. There are other ways to save money, however, and here they are:

1. *Borrow from friends*—Many people exchange maternity outfits. Keep notes of what belongs to whom and make sure they're returned, cleaned, and pressed, within three months after your baby is born. You can also raid your husband's closet for some loose-fitting items.

2. *Improvise*—Some of your regular dresses can be worn unbelted. Or empire-line and tent dresses will fill the bill for several months. Buy a well-cut pair of pants and a skirt in a dark color. Use your drawstring pants instead of maternity. Wear long, elastic waist skirts to hide your swollen ankles.

3. *Don't remove price tags*—Keep price tags on nursing bras until your milk comes in. Only then will you know whether they fit and are comfortable.

4. *Internet*—There's a thriving market for secondhand maternity wear on the Internet.

5. *Travel to an outlet store*—These stores will save you anywhere from 25–90 percent off retail prices. Don't forget to take a peek into large discount stores like Wal-Mart or Target.

6. *Use consignment stores*—Get to know the people in a consignment store. Ask them to call you when some nice maternity outfits come in.

7. *Look for used items in ads*—Check newspaper classified ads and garage sales. After giving birth, some women can't wait to sell their perfectly good maternity clothes for a song (or a lullaby).

8. *Make some maternity clothes*—A wide variety of patterns are available for maternity clothes. Some women find this a relaxing activity in the evening. Look at the clothes in maternity shops to see how manufacturers use elastic inserts, tabs, and Velcro strips for expansion techniques you can use.

Storing Maternity Clothes Properly

Once your first baby comes along, there are often others to follow. Save your nicest maternity clothes to wear the next time you're pregnant. Here are some storage tips:

• Clean everything before storing, including the storage space. Dirty clothing attracts moths and other insects.

• Use cedar chests, airtight containers, and sealed cardboard boxes for storage. Never use plastic. It holds moisture and may cause mildew to form.

• Put containers in a cool, well-ventilated area, such as a large, dark closet (light may cause colors to fade). Avoid areas with extreme temperatures and humidity.

- Use mothballs or lavender-scented sachets. Although they don't kill moth eggs that are already in your woolen clothes, they do work as a repellent. Keep your nonwool clothes smelling fresh by wrapping fragrant potpourri in netting and placing between sheets of tissue.

- If you prefer to store clothes by hanging in a closet, drape a sheet over everything to keep out dust and light.

Chapter 6

Working with Your Birth Specialist

As a pregnant working woman, you need to make choices that are compatible with your job responsibilities and yet will bring you the birth experience you want. There are a number of time-saving ways to do this, including conducting initial telephone interviews and preparing ahead of time for in-person interviews. The first step, however, is to understand your options.

When weighing all of your options, three factors you should consider are:

1. *Location*—In part, your choice of doctor/birth attendant will depend on your place of employment and residence. You'll be having frequent checkups during your pregnancy; choosing someone close to work will be a convenience, especially if you plan to work until your due date. Look into the choices available even if you've been going to the same gynecologist for years.

2. *Employer Benefits*—Check your employer-provided health insurance early on in your pregnancy for approved doctors and for pregnancy benefits, such as maternity leave. Also, check the coverage for pregnancy and birth expenses, which vary from policy to policy. Is there a waiting period before coverage begins? Does it say how much you'll have to cover out of pocket? How is payment handled for services? How many hospital days do they allow for a vaginal birth and a Caesarean birth (see "Childbirth Costs Worksheet," page 195)?

3. *Cost*—The fees of obstetricians, family physicians, and midwives vary so greatly that you must be armed with all the facts, including costs, before making a decision.

FYI: Who is Delivering Babies?

The National Center for Health Statistics reports that physicians delivered 97 percent of hospital births in the '80s and '90s. Midwives attended to approximately 3 percent of all hospital and home births. In the 2000s, midwives continued to deliver more babies, although the percentage is still small.

DOCTOR/BIRTH ATTENDANT ESTIMATE WORKSHEET

Description of Services   **Cost**

1. Name_____   _____

Address _____

City _____

Phone _____

Nurse_____

Ref'd by _____

Comments _____

_____

_____

_____

2. Name_____   _____

Address _____

City _____

Phone _____

Nurse_____

Ref'd by _____

Comments _____

_____

_____

_____

3. Name_____   _____

Address _____

City _____

Phone _____

Nurse_____

Ref'd by _____

Comments _____

_____

_____

_____

Name of Selected Obstetrician/Midwife: _____

Address _____

City _____

Zip_____

Total Cost _____

Hours_____

Emergency phone _____

Extra Costs _____

Insurance reimbursement_____

Notes: _____

_____

_____

_____

Guaranteeing a Successful Prenatal Checkup

One of your challenges as an expectant career woman is to schedule doctor visits around your job. You can be sure that (a) your time is spent productively, (b) waiting time is shortened, and (c) examination time is limited by following these simple steps:

1. *Plan appointments around your work agenda*—Schedule your appointment the first thing in the morning (so you're not kept waiting), during your lunch break, or make it the last appointment of the day so that you won't miss much, if any, time from work. You may even be able to schedule an appointment on the weekend.

2. *Call ahead to see if the doctor is running late*—Call one half to one hour in advance and ask if the doctor is running on time. If the answer is no, get a little extra work done before you leave the office. Ask a friendly receptionist to call you when she knows the doctor is running behind time.

3. *If the doctor is regularly late for your appointments, talk about your frustration*—Explain that as a working woman, your time is money too. Consider asking for a reduction in the fee for every fifteen minutes you're kept waiting. Or, if worse comes to worse, threaten to switch doctors if an effort is not made to see you on time.

4. *Use waiting time for information-gathering*—Instead of letting the

delay upset you, talk to the other waiting expectant mothers about their experiences and the wisdom they've gained. Somehow, knowing that almost all women go through the same experiences is reassuring.

5. *Bring work along*—Use the time for office work, a home project, or bill paying.

6. *List your questions*—Write them in order of priority because you may not have time for all of them. Make them specific and scientifically current to be sure the doctor appreciates your concerns.

7. *Call with some questions*—Your concern may be easier to answer than you think, saving everybody's time.

Six Tips for Calling Your Doctor from Work

1. *Keep numbers handy*—All your records, the doctor's phone number, and the pharmacist's phone number should be within reach at work. By the time you get home, they may have closed or you may have forgotten the question.

2. *Make the call yourself*—Messages relayed through a coworker have the potential for error.

3. *Call when you're free*—Avoid calling just before a meeting or when a

presentation is scheduled. By the time the doctor calls back, you may be unavailable, wasting everybody's time.

4. *Identify yourself*—Always give the receptionist your full name, date of your last appointment, and your current week of pregnancy.

5. *Give details*—For example, say how much bleeding occurred (how many pads you bled through), what it looked like, and so forth. The nurse may be able to set your mind at ease or may be able to connect you directly with the doctor.

6. *Keep paper and pencil handy*—You may get complicated instructions. (As an added reminder, call home and leave your doctor's medical instructions on your voicemail.)

PERSONAL PREGNANCY DIARY

My Healthcare Team

Doctor's/Midwife's name: _____

Doctor's/Midwife's address: _____

Nurses: _____

Emergency Service number(s): _____

Receptionist: _____

Pediatrician's Name: _____

Telephone answering service: _____

Address: _____

_____

Childbirth Education

Educator: _____

Beginning date: _____

Place: _____

Ending date: _____

Telephone: _____

Comments/Observations: _____

_____

_____

_____

_____

Medical Data

Medications Taken: _____

Dose: _____

Date Started: _____

Date Ended: _____

Allergies: _____

Vital Statistics

Prepregnant weight:_____ lbs.

Last menstrual period: _____

Blood type: _____

Rh factor: _____

Rubella status: _____

Special Tests

Date: _____

Procedure: _____

Reason: _____

Findings: _____

PRENATAL APPOINTMENT CALENDAR

Visit: _____

Date: _____

Time: _____

Weeks: _____

Weight: _____

1st _____

Questions/Comments _____

_____

_____

2nd _____

Questions/Comments _____

_____

_____

3rd _____

Questions/Comments _____

_____

_____

4th _____

Questions/Comments _____

_____

_____

5th _____

Questions/Comments _____

_____

_____

6th _____

Questions/Comments _____

_____

_____

7th _____

Questions/Comments _____

_____

_____

8th _____

Questions/Comments _____

_____

_____

9th_____

Questions/Comments _____

_____

_____

10th_____

Questions/Comments _____

_____

_____

11th_____

Questions/Comments _____

_____

_____

12th_____

Questions/Comments _____

_____

_____

13th_____

Questions/Comments _____

_____

_____

Part Two

Planning Ahead for the Working Woman

Chapter 7

Announcing Your Pregnancy to Your Boss and Coworkers

Good relations between employer and employee and among coworkers are significant factors in any job. You can't get your work done as promptly and efficiently with a cloud of resentment and anger hanging over your head. For some reason, a pregnant woman raises some people's hackles, especially the boss's, who sometimes feels that becoming pregnant somehow indicates a lack of devotion to the job. Announcing your condition must be approached, in many cases, with caution.

Telling the Boss You're Pregnant

Two people have to feel reassured after you break the news that you're pregnant—you and your supervisor. You're worried about the safety of your expected child, the financial stability of your family, and your own self-esteem, which is often closely tied to your job. Your employer, on the other hand, has other concerns: Will the business suffer? Will you give the same attention to your work with a baby at home to worry about? It's important that you consider the concerns of your employer and follow these suggestions:

1. *Don't announce your pregnancy until after the first trimester, when the risk of miscarriage is much lower*—The longer you wait, the less time there is for office speculation about your future. Don't wait until you show, however, because coworkers are apt to notice first. Of course, if you're suffering from morning sickness, or if you're asked to take on a long-term project, you'll have to explain. Tell close friends at work who can keep your secret and a few select people on the been-there/done-that list who can share strategic advice about how to tell the big cheese.

2. *Tell your employer next*—It would not be to your benefit to have your boss hear the news from someone else. Your negotiating position could be weakened. So tell your boss after you do your legwork, before you begin to show, and before someone else can. If your employer learns about your pregnancy before you have a chance to tell him, explain that you wanted to get your prenatal test results back first to make sure everything was going well. Then you were going to make an appointment to discuss a rough plan for covering all your responsibilities during your leave.

3. *Choose your moment*—Pick the least stressful, most convenient time, perhaps a Friday afternoon. Certainly you would never do it before an important event, such as a major stockholder meeting.

4. *Speak in private*—Arrange not to be interrupted during the conversation. If you choose a restaurant, make sure it's quiet and low key. Discourage any over-diligent waiter.

5. *Be positive*—Be forthright and optimistic. You want to give the impression that you have everything organized, yet you remain flexible. Never apologize, even if you're aware that you will be leaving your position in the middle of the spring rush, or the fall sales season. Don't say you're sorry. You haven't done anything wrong; you're just having a baby.

6. *Discuss your pregnancy in a business-like manner*—Emphasize the temporary nature of the situation. Underline your enthusiasm for your work and your determination to be as productive as ever.

7. *Don't discuss maternity leave yet*—Wait awhile and schedule a formal meeting to discuss the details of your leave and your future with the company. In the meantime, contact the U.S. Equal Employment Opportunity Commission and your state civil rights commission to find out what your rights are (see "Understanding the Leave Laws and Policies," page 107).

8. *Assume you'll be welcomed back*—Never ask whether you may come back. Take it for granted that you will (see "Managing Your Maternity Leave," page 106).

9. *Tell coworkers*—Making it clear after the initial hoopla and congrats that you're working out a plan for your leave won't leave them in a panic.

10. *Let customers, clients, and any outside vendors or consultants know*—This can wait, especially if you don't have regular face-to-face meetings with them. Assure them that their needs will be met and any necessary transitions will be handled smoothly.

FYI: Working Women Come Back to Their Jobs

Studies have shown that almost 90 percent of the women who go on maternity leave eventually return to their jobs. Of those women, 43 percent return within three months.

Making a Smooth Transition

The first step for good workplace relations is to treat your employer and coworkers with respect and understanding—basically, the two most important things you want and need from them during and after your pregnancy. For example:

- *Cooperate*—Develop an attitude of mutual support among your peers by pitching in during vacations and sick days.

- *Reciprocate*—Always be quick to return favors. If someone covers for you when you visit the obstetrician, make sure you make up the time within the next week. Be generous with thanks and appreciation;

sometimes a little gift is appropriate. Better yet, build up a bank of favors with your coworkers that you can draw on when needed.

• *Don't complain about how you feel or how busy you are*—Nobody wants to listen to someone moan about their situation, especially if they have been given a new, easier work arrangement.

• *Stay on top of your workload during your pregnancy*—Don't get behind. If possible, get ahead on some duties. Never expect an associate to take over some of your work because you're in this new condition.

• *Talk things over*—Discuss your anticipated leave with your colleagues and address any questions, or problems, they may have. Remember, they may not be looking forward to the changes when you're absent. Keep any doubts about returning after your leave to yourself. Don't forget to let contacts and clients know when you'll be leaving and who'll be handling your work while you're away.

• *Change your voicemail message and reroute your mail*—Find out who will be handling your mail while you're gone. When recording your out-of-office voicemail message, include the length of your absence, the approximate date you expect to return, and the name and number of the person(s) covering for you. Set up an automatic email reply with the same information.

- *Train your replacement well*—Don't wait until the last minute to discuss your replacement. Find out if you're expected to find and train him. If your colleagues are expected to pitch in and help, start long-term projects before you leave and hand off smaller tasks to other workers. Never withhold any information from your substitute out of anxiety about being replaced. When you've trained that person very well, the flow of work will not be interrupted, and you will get the credit.

- *Trust your replacement*—Once you have delegated your work or trained your replacement, be prepared to let her do the job. If you continually call or pop into the office unannounced attempting to check up on her, you could cause confusion and resentment.

- *Put your desk in order*—Organize your files, reports, and other material that will be needed while you're away. Create a clearly labeled folder with contact information, file locations, and other relevant information.

- *Clean your virtual desk*—Plan to leave a tidy computer behind you, particularly if supervisors and coworkers will have access to it while you're on leave. Remove any personal files and even remotely inappropriate documents. Make sure your files your coworkers will need during your absence are easy to access and understand. Create a master list detailing how your files are organized and make a hard copy of this master list. Make copies of important folders and files; back up copies for the workplace on floppies or CD-RW, and make an extra copy you can take home if you need to access it while you're out. Don't forget to pass on your passwords.

- *Stay in touch*—Call once or twice to catch up on the latest office talk. Toward the end of your leave, make arrangements to call in once a week. Be available by cell phone for emergencies. Accept calls from work. Designate a contact person at your office and try to have all office communications go through him at regularly scheduled times to give you and your family as much privacy and rest as possible. Ask that copies of memos, mail, and other important correspondence be sent to you. Let everybody know that you'll be back soon.

Strategies for Dealing with Difficult Coworkers

Not everyone will be thrilled with the news of your pregnancy. Conflicts between associates stem from many sources; among them is a belief that a working mother will have family problems that conflict with work performance, a feeling of jealousy over perceived special treatment, or a belief that mothers, or expectant mothers, belong in the home. The trick is to try to manage people's reactions and their treatment of you.

Practically speaking, you need your coworkers' cooperation to accomplish your job. A hostile associate could cut you out of the loop or "forget" to give you phone messages with the result that your clients or superiors might begin to think you're unresponsive or worse, incompetent. The time and energy you would devote to such a conflict could be much better spent on improving your production.

The best way to control the situation, as with any management issue, is to be proactive. If you sense any newfound tension, here are some suggestions:

- *Investigate*—There's always the possibility that you are at fault. Perhaps you're making errors that someone else has had to correct because you're preoccupied with your pregnancy or approaching parenthood. Or you may have been unintentionally abrupt with coworkers. Ask a trusted colleague to explain what's wrong.

- *Clear the air*—Set up a private meeting with each person involved in the conflict. Approach the discussion in a matter-of-fact, neutral manner. Keep your voice free of emotion, and your coworker might realize that his or her emotions might be intensifying the conflict. You're not there to point fingers or defend your position, but to find a solution to a problem that is disrupting the workplace. State your experience as nonjudgmentally as possible. Then give your colleague a chance to respond without interruption. Bite your tongue if you have to, but listen carefully with respect to the other person's point of view. Demonstrate your willingness to adapt.

- *Consult your boss*—Only as a last resort should you discuss the matter with your superior. Perhaps an adjustment in your duties will ease the tension. Be careful on this step—it could backfire. The people who are resentful of you now may only harden their attitude if they feel the boss is taking your side.

It is always wiser to avoid conflicts than to try and solve them once they've occurred. And sometimes you just have to accept the things you can't change. Some people may never be easy to deal with. You just have to evaluate the advantages and disadvantages of your job and decide which ones outweigh others.

Many pregnant women experience having their tummies rubbed by strangers who do it because they are just unthinking and don't realize they're being rude. Try to understand the point of view or the motivation of the people saying or doing offensive or stupid things. Although a sarcastic response may be on the tip of your tongue, humor mixed with information is usually a more effective approach in the long run.

Be firm with people who are genuinely offensive or whose actions constitute harassment. Ask them politely to stop and tell them it makes you uncomfortable, or gently guide their hands off your belly. You'll have to adjust the response to the situation—for example, when it's your boss or an important client—but don't snap back. It'll make you look unprofessional. (See "What to Do When You Suspect Bias Based on Your Pregnancy," page 113.)

Here are five ways to say "none of your business" to unsolicited advice:

1. That's something my husband/partner/doctor/midwife has already worked out.

2. Thank you for your concern.

3. I'd rather not talk about it.

4. My, that's awfully personal!

5. What a question!

Chapter 8

Managing Your Maternity Leave

A United Nations survey found that out of one hundred and fifty-two countries, the United States, Australia, New Zealand, Lesotho, Switzerland, and Papua New Guinea were the only ones one that did not have a national policy requiring paid maternity leave. The majority of countries surveyed provide benefits through social welfare systems, some require the employer to pay, and still others combine both financing sources.

Out of the millions of working women in this country, only one-third of those are working for businesses that have a maternity leave policy and 50 percent have to take their leave without pay, or use a mixed bag of time off from vacation, short-term disability, parental leave, or sick leave.

While it's important for you to be aware of the implications if you're fortunate enough to work for a company with a maternity leave policy, you should also understand your legal rights under state and federal laws in this area. Federal regulations do not guarantee your right to a maternity leave under certain qualifications, and state regulations are not consistent throughout the United States. What is guaranteed is your right to a disability leave if your company has disability leave for other medical situations.

Understanding the Leave Laws and Policies

In order to make sure that you are being treated fairly and getting all the leave benefits to which you are entitled, it is critical that you understand the following laws and policies:

The Civil Rights Act of 1964

Under the Civil Rights Act, unwelcome sexual advances, requests for sexual favors, and other verbal or physical conduct of a sexual nature constitute sexual harassment when submission to or rejection of this conduct explicitly or implicitly affects an individual's employment, unreasonably interferes with an individual's work performance, or creates an intimidating, hostile or offensive work environment.

The Pregnancy Discrimination Act of 1978

This amendment to the Civil Rights Act of 1964 was the first piece of federal legislation that stated clearly you cannot be fired for being pregnant.

- Applies to companies with fifteen or more employees.

- Treats pregnancy, pregnancy-related illnesses, and childbirth on an equal basis with all other medical conditions or short-term disabilities. If, for example, your company offers disability benefits, sick leave, or health insurance to other workers while they're on disability leave, they cannot be denied to you because you're pregnant.

• Employers cannot refuse to hire or promote you, force you to go on leave, or deny you fringe benefits, such as vacation days, seniority credit, or pay increases, while you're on maternity leave.

• If you are temporarily unable to perform your job due to pregnancy, your employer must treat you the same as any other temporarily disabled employee; for example, by providing modified tasks, alternative assignments, disability leave, or leave without pay.

• You must be permitted to work as long as you are able to perform your job.

• If you have been absent from work as a result of a pregnancy-related condition, and you recover, your employer may not require you to remain on leave until your baby's birth.

• Your employer may not have a rule that prohibits you from returning to work for a predetermined length of time after childbirth. And your employer must hold open a job for a pregnancy-related absence the same length of time jobs are held open for employees on sick or disability leave.

The National Family and Medical Leave Act of 1993

Basic Provisions

Fortunately, with the passage of the National Family and Medical Leave Act (FMLA) of 1993, benefits and protection for working families got better.

1. Applies to companies with fifty or more employees.

2. Allows up to twelve weeks of unpaid leave each year to care for a newborn or adopted child; or a sick child, spouse, or parent; and for personal illness.

3. Employees must be given their original position or comparable job upon return.

4. Employers must continue to provide health benefits for employees on leave.

5. Applies to workers who have been employed full-time for one year or to part-time employees who have worked at least 1,250 hours in the previous twelve months.

6. Teachers may be asked to remain on leave until the next school term under certain conditions related to the school calendar.

Business Provisions

1. Exempts companies with fewer than fifty workers.

2. Lets companies deny the benefit to salaried employees within the highest-paid 10 percent of their workforce, if letting the workers take the leave would create "substantial and grievous injury" to the business operations.

3. Permits employers to obtain up to three medical opinions and certifications on the need for the leave.

4. If workers do not come back, employers can recapture the healthcare premiums they paid during the leave.

How the FMLA works

The FMLA doesn't require the leave to be taken by the week or even by the day. If you have an illness that requires treatment several times a week, you could conceivably take your FMLA leave in hour-long blocks. Even though that could drive your employer crazy, if the situation demands it, they are obligated to approve. It's smart to work out a schedule, when possible, that reduces the impact on your employer.

Alert your physician to the situation and ask for help in minimizing the medically necessary leave. Your company's personnel department may be an ally. By giving that office permission to contact your doctor, the official HR spokesperson can have more success than you in getting medical appointments at convenient times.

The law also says that unless the situation is an emergency, you have to give your employer at least thirty days notice that you intend to use FMLA benefits. To minimize resentment created by understaffing, do what you can to make your absence no big deal.

FYI: Both employers and employees say the FMLA is making things better!

Many larger firms actually reported cost savings related to FMLA, mostly from reduced employee turnover and training, and increased productivity and morale. A simple, user-friendly edition of the FMLA can be found on the website of the National Partnership for Women and Families at www.nationalpartnership.org. To inquire by phone, call (800) 669-4000.

State Laws for Maternity Leave

In 1987, the U.S. Supreme Court ruled that every state has the right to enact antidiscrimination laws to protect pregnant employees. About half the states have enacted laws since then requiring all but the smallest companies to give unpaid leave to pregnant workers. The standard paid maternity/disability leave, which must be certified by a physician, is six to eight weeks plus any accrued vacation time, with the average leave being three months. Sometimes, it's extended for a Caesarean birth.

In many cases, firms must promise the same job, or a comparable one, after the leave has ended. According to federal law, any greater right allowed by state law prevails. Contact your state labor board or employment office for more information.

If your employer doesn't have a disability plan—often the case with a small business—you may have to accept an unpaid leave (see "Budget Strategies," page 189). In that case, check with your local employment office to find out if you're qualified for unemployment benefits or temporary state disability benefits. Also, a few very progressive companies offer parental leave, which is usually in addition to maternity/disability leave and is available to both men and women.

Paternity Leave

Even though the FMLA provides new parents—including fathers and adoptive parents—with twelve weeks of unpaid leave to care for a newborn or adopted child, the myth is still around that men who take paternity leave are not serious about their jobs. Also, companies usually don't encourage new fathers to take time off for bonding with a new child.

While 50 percent of all fathers questioned in a national survey said they would spend more time with their children if their jobs permitted, they're more likely to take vacation time or use sick days when their babies are born. That's because they are afraid their managers or coworkers will disapprove. Only 15 percent of men eligible under FMLA make a formal request for paternity leave.

Given a choice between paternity leave or more flexible work arrangements such as telecommuting, most fathers voted for the latter. That's why an increasing number of companies offer benefits such as flexible work arrangements, parenting education classes, and on-site child care.

What to Do When You Suspect Bias Based on Your Pregnancy

Discrimination can occur in many different forms. Under the aforementioned laws, the following subtle and not-so-subtle types of pregnancy and sex discrimination are also prohibited:

Hiring Practices

- An employer refused to hire you because of your pregnancy-related condition even though you were able to perform the major functions of the job.

- An employer refused to hire you because of his or her prejudices against pregnant workers or the prejudices of coworkers, clients, or customers.

- An employer asked you about future plans that you may have for pregnancy during an interview or after you're hired.

Job Duties

- Certain job responsibilities you were able to perform were assigned to another coworker.

- You were not provided modified tasks or alternative assignments when you were temporarily unable to perform your job while other temporarily disabled employees at your workplace were.

- Your employer singled out pregnancy-related conditions for special procedures to determine your ability to work. (If, however, your employer requires its employees to submit a doctor's statement concerning their inability to work before granting leave or paying sick benefits, your employer may require you to submit such statements.)

- Your well-earned raise had been denied.

- You were given a poor job performance evaluation for no good reason.

- Your employer made sexist comments about your "crazy" hormones or expanding belly or made unwelcome sexual advances or requests.

Fringe Benefits
- Pregnancy-related benefits are limited because you are unmarried.

- Benefits are provided for other medical conditions, but not for pregnancy-related conditions.

- Benefits are provided to workers on leave, but not for those on leave for pregnancy-related conditions.

- You are not treated the same as other temporarily disabled employees for accrual and crediting of seniority, vacation calculation, pay increases, and temporary disability benefits.

If you feel you are treated badly on the job because you are pregnant, there are several steps you can take to remedy the situation:

- *Stand up for yourself*—In a dignified way, make it clear to your boss that "punishment" for having a child is against the law.

- *Keep a written record*—Document any negative comments or insulting behavior regarding your pregnancy. Keep detailed notes on everything, plus copies of all relevant interoffice memos. Get a copy of your personnel file, if possible, and photocopy any past performance reviews. Find out if anyone else in your workplace has experienced similar problems.

- *Seek relief higher up*—Go through whatever channels are necessary to stop the discrimination: your union, your human resources, the personnel department, or your boss's supervisor. Employers are obligated by law to take steps necessary to prevent discrimination from occurring. These include clearly communicating to employees that discrimination or sexual harassment will not be tolerated and by establishing an effective complaint or grievance process and taking immediate and appropriate action when an employee complains.

- *Stay abreast of current laws*—A coalition of civil rights groups is lobbying for new legislation to strengthen the civil rights laws. To get more information about what you're legally entitled to, contact:

- 9to5, National Association of Working Women
  (800) 522-0925

- National Partnership for Women and Families
  (202) 986-2600

- U.S. Department of Labor
  (800) 827-5335

- The Employment Law Guide
  (866) 4USADOL

- *File a complaint*—If nothing else works, and you're prepared to spend at least eighteen months fighting your case and possibly suffering career repercussions, file a complaint with one of the following:

  - American Civil Liberties Union

  - Commission on Human Rights

  - Department of Fair Employment and Housing

  - The Equal Employment Opportunity Commission

  - National Woman's Law Center

- Women's Legal Defense Fund

- Women's Rights Agency of the State

- Check into the many websites for interviewing about dealing with the "illegal question"

If it is decided that you are indeed being discriminated against, you would be entitled to a remedy that would place you in the position you would have been in if the discrimination had never occurred. You may be entitled to hiring, promotion, reinstatement, back pay, and other remuneration. Some state and local laws do allow damages to compensate you for future pecuniary losses, mental anguish, and inconvenience. Punitive damages may be available, as well, if your employer acted with malice or reckless indifference. You may also be entitled to attorney's fees.

Planning Your Maternity Leave

Before you begin negotiating your maternity leave, you need to do the following important things first:

- *Begin planning early*—As soon as you know you're pregnant, start musing about the responsibilities. Don't hesitate to toss out ideas and ponder new ones. The initial confusion will eventually sort itself out, and you'll be clearer about the way to go. Jot down ideas as they come to you. Refer to your notes often until you decide whether your idea has merit.

- *Research your organization*—Get a read on the culture of your company by talking to people who have successfully negotiated flexible work arrangements for themselves. Know your supervisor and your negotiating position in the company.

- *Check your office manual for flexible work policies and review their provisions thoroughly*—Research your company's literature to study your employer's mission statements, company credos, and consider how you can pull the language in these statements for possible inclusion into your written proposal.

- *Review your company's short-term disability and medical policies*—You should search for anything that strikes you as treating pregnancy as any different from any other short-term disability. (Some disability plans will provide for a paid leave to begin two to four weeks before your due date. That would give you time to tie up the loose ends, arrange the baby's room, or just relax.) Of course, your company may have a specific maternity leave policy, so be sure to study that as well.

Find out specifically what paid and unpaid leave you are eligible for. You might have some leave without pay that still includes benefits (usually a combination of your company's maternity leave policy, a short-term disability program, and accrued time off). Add up your accumulated vacation, sick, and personal days, and determine just how much unpaid leave your finances will allow. (Keep in mind when budgeting that your employer can legally require you to use up your paid leave first, and that some states require you to cover at least a portion of your leave before disability kicks in.) Again, check with your state labor office to learn about disability options. This is particularly important if you are working in a smaller company.

• *Review your work performance since your last job evaluation*—You will want to show two things: First, that you can and have done the job, even through you're pregnant. Second, you want to pay attention so that when the employer starts to reduce your duties, you can document the change. Then make an appointment with your human resources department and let them know about your pregnancy.

• *Talk to someone who understands your company's policy*—Your personnel officer, union representative, human resources department, or office manager will know the answers to your questions. Larger companies will have the facts, in writing, usually in the employee's handbook. You are legally entitled to look at it without having to say why or to specify what policy or policies you're reviewing. Many companies also have this information on the Internet. The smaller your company, the less likely it is to have an official policy (see "What to Do If Your Employer Does Not Have a Maternity Leave Policy," page 130). You may discover that no policy exists because it's preferred to provide a general leave negotiated on an individual bias.

• *Gather intelligence*—Talk to several other women in the firm who have gone on maternity leave. They can tell you whether obtaining your rights will be easy or a struggle. Discreetly ask them how they managed to strike a deal. Assuming that a maternity leave policy does exist, your guiding principle in considering it is a simple question: is it made more difficult for pregnant women than for disabled employees? If your company allows employees to return to the job after a heart attack, or an injury from a car accident, or continues their pay while they heal, then it must provide at least the same terms for your disability leave.

• *Approach the meeting in a matter-of-fact way and avoid any antagonistic statements*—The person you're meeting with wants to inform you, not to argue about an already established policy. Use the worksheet that follows to document the facts about your company's maternity leave policy.

MATERNITY LEAVE POLICY WORKSHEET

Benefits Manager's Name: (Union Representative/Personnel Director)

_____

1. Is a paid maternity/paternity/parental leave available?_____

    For how long and at what rate of pay? _____

    What are the eligibility requirements? _____

    _____

    What is the procedure to request a leave? _____

    _____

    _____

    What percentage of salary does a disability plan pay?_____

    How long will my commissions continue?_____

    Will I receive full commission or a percentage? _____

    Can I take off time during my pregnancy without losing maternity leave?
    (This is important because you may become temporarily ill in the later
    months or you may simply need time to get ready.) _____

2. Is an unpaid maternity/paternity/parental leave available?_____

    For how long?_____

    What are the eligibility requirements? _____

    _____

    _____

What benefits are provided during leave? _____

_____

_____

At what point will my benefits be affected?_____

If I take unpaid leave, will I retain the same position, wages, and seniority?

_____

3. Can I extend my leave by taking:

Accrued sick leave?	Paid	Unpaid
Accrued vacation time?	Paid	Unpaid
Personal days?	Paid	Unpaid

What must I do to file for an extension of leave? _____

_____

_____

4. Which of the following are protected if I extend my leave:

Salary?_____

Seniority benefits? _____

Position I hold now? _____

Similar position?_____

What is the procedure if I decide to come back early? _____

_____

_____

Are there other options? (Perhaps you can take an additional six months with the stipulation that you will not be guaranteed your same position.)

_____

_____

_____

_____

Other questions or concerns:_____

_____

_____

_____

Special instructions for how work is to be handled during my absence: _____

_____

_____

_____

If my firm has no leave policy, these are the agreed-upon details of my leave:

_____

_____

_____

_____

Negotiating the Maternity Leave You Want

How much leave your employer will allow and how much you want will most likely differ. Many companies are now using a sliding scale for maternity leave, based on seniority and length of time an employee has been with the company. Although, realistically speaking, it will be difficult to know for certain until your baby is born, you must do your best now to choose the right maternity leave for you.

Successful bargainers know that negotiation is a compromise. There must be something each party wants in the final agreement. The hour and setting of the meeting are significant factors, as are your employer's personality and management style. Be sure to listen carefully to everything that's said, especially the objections, and watch body language. Always remain professional; emotions don't belong in a negotiating sessions. No matter what the results are, always thank your supervisor for his or her time.

Follow these steps to insure a successful negotiating session:

- *Make an appointment*—Don't ever drop in unannounced. State the purpose of the meeting in advance so that your boss will be prepared for the discussion. Make sure to pick a quiet time of day. If the office is never quiet, consider going to a restaurant.

- *Establish your value to the firm*—The more valuable you are, the more bargaining power you will have. You must convince your supervisor of your importance to the company by reviewing promotions you've received and your specific contributions to the company. Prepare yourself by making a list of your assets and memorizing them. Tell your boss that giving you what you want benefits the company; your skills and experience make you a valuable employee, and your company could easily lose more time and money by letting you go.

- *Handle the meeting as a professional*—Speak in a non-demanding and positive voice. Stress the benefit to the company of cooperating with a valued employee. State your proposal in a confident way; for example, "I propose a cost-saving approach to retaining my training and experience that will also lead to an increase in on-the-job (select: productivity, concentration, energy, loyalty, efficiency, creativity, etc.)."

- *Emphasize that you want and plan to return*—Assure your boss that you'll be back to work after your leave; there'll be no need to find a permanent replacement. Stress your commitment to your job. If you want a different work arrangement after your leave, this is the time to discuss it (see "Work Options to Consider When Your Maternity Leave Ends," page 132.

- *Keep your leaving date open*—Try to keep the beginning date for your leave as flexible as possible. (Remember, the due date is the actual birth date for only one in ten babies, and passing it by two weeks is not uncommon.) You may feel very fit and healthy up to the last minute and want to avoid being bored waiting at home. If you want to stay at work until labor begins, ask your doctor to certify your expected delivery date two weeks beyond your fortieth week.

- *Ask for more than you expect to get*—Tack on four to six weeks to your initial supplemental leave request so that there's room for compromise. If you get the maximum you request without need for compromise, take it. You can always return to work earlier if your finances require it. Dr. T. Berry Brazelton, one of America's leading pediatricians, strongly recommends at least a four-month maternity leave. He believes that new parents need that time to get to know their baby. Additionally, most babies have settled into a routine by then, are over their fussy time, and are sleeping through the night (not an insignificant point for working parents). Clearly, your maternity leave should not end until you're physically and emotionally ready. It takes a minimum of six weeks for you to regain your energy. And at least two months are needed for establishing a breast-feeding routine, finding good child care, and adjusting to the greatest life change of all. No matter how much time you take off, your transition back to work will be easier if your partner will take a leave that overlaps your first days back in the workplace.

- *Provide good solutions to your boss's problems*—Because your employer's first thoughts will be about the impact on the business, come prepared with a well-thought-out plan for shifting your responsibilities to others; e.g., delegate your work to previously trained staff; hire a recently retired professional; use a professional temp agency; get a graduate student in the field or a student intern; cross-train a coworker, staff person, or junior employee. Reassure your employer that you'll be available by whatever electronic means the company chooses: fax, voicemail, telephone, or pager. The fact of your availability will be more important than the need to contact you. Have a trusted colleague, family, or friend review your work coverage plan before presenting it to your boss.

• *Think through your arguments*—Write the proposal to benefit your supervisor while at the same time giving careful consideration to your priorities in your personal, financial, and professional life. Expect objections and have solutions ready. If you want to work part-time, mention that you can identify and eliminate 20 percent of your workload and are willing to take a 20 percent reduction in pay. Or when you telecommute, there will be improved productivity due to fewer interruptions and no commute time. If you want to work a compressed work week, tell your boss there will be better coverage during extended hours of certain days. Or he or she will save physical space when you and someone else share a desk and telecommute or work part-time on opposite days. Citing flexible work arrangements within your profession and/or industry (especially with competitors) can also be effective.

• *Give your boss a role*—Even if you have the plan all worked out, it doesn't hurt to find a way for your boss to have some input. Present your plan and ask how he or she thinks this will work out in your department. Tell your supervisor you can make adjustments to this plan as necessary should circumstances change. Treat it like a proposal that is open to negotiation. The better your plan assures your boss that your work will get done, the more cooperation and flexibility you're likely to encounter.

- *Have a substitute plan ready*—Show your willingness to be flexible by preparing a second leave plan to present if the first one meets resistance. Under FMLA, you can break up your twelve weeks in any way. For instance, you can take eight weeks up front and then spread the next four over several shortened work weeks before returning full-time. Your employer will likely be amendable to this idea, as she or he will surely be eager to get you back into the office as soon as possible.

Remember, your significant other is also entitled to take a twelve-week FMLA leave with the arrival of your child (see "Paternity Leave," page 112). Unless you work for the same employer, you can each take up to twelve weeks at the same time, you can overlap a portion of your leaves, or you can take them consecutively, as long as each leave occurs within a year of your child's birth. (Your partner, of course, will not be entitled to any medical disability pay.) You may be able to arrange for your partner to care for your baby during your initial weeks back at work, which would no doubt make the transition a much easier one for you.

- *At the first meeting, accept the points you've agreed on and leave*—Now that you know your employer's objections to other points, you'll be able to develop new ideas to be discussed at another meeting. Don't rush into anything; once you announce an early decision, either you're stuck with it or you look indecisive to your colleagues if you change it. Much of your decision will depend on your level of energy, the progression of your pregnancy, and the kind of work you do.

• *Suggest a trial period*—That way you and your supervisor can review the arrangement and make adjustments if needed.

• *Don't be pressured into accepting an unsuitable leave plan*—If you're presented with a leave plan that is clearly unacceptable, say that you'll need time to think it over and make another appointment. Don't let your superior force you into an arrangement that's bad for you and your family. Say nicely but firmly, "In fact, I am planning to take the full twelve weeks offered by federal law. Here's the plan I've drawn up." If your boss is really uncertain about what the law provides, tell him or her you'll be happy to provide an update and bring a copy of the office's policy. Remember, you're not asking for approval, but anything you can do to make your supervisor better informed, especially about the law, will benefit both you and other moms-to-be who follow in your footsteps. If it just doesn't seem to be working, see "Work Options to Consider," page 132.

• *Document everything*—Keep a written record of all the points agreed upon (see "Sample Maternity Leave Agreement," page 138), or write a memo covering everything. Sign it, date it, and have your boss do the same. Keep a copy for yourself, of course, give a copy to your boss, and give another one to the personnel department.

What to Do If Your Employer Does Not Have a Maternity Leave Policy

If your research has uncovered the absence of any maternity leave policy in your company, you may have to argue first for a policy before you consider negotiating for a leave. Begin by checking out what comparable organizations do for their employees so you can assess the likelihood of getting what you want and frame arguments in support of your position.

Next, try to gather support by asking what others think. Try to gauge the level of demand for the policy you have in mind. Approach the right person. Speak with a supervisor. If you're part of a collective bargaining agreement, talk to your union representative.

Don't give up when the answer is no. It may take a long time to plant the seed about a family-friendly policy, but eventually a groundswell of support for the idea will grow, and responsive management may then be more willing to consider your concerns. When arguing your case, the following benefits to the company should be covered:

1. *Morale*—So many women have flooded into the marketplace (and even more are now attending college) that no firm can expect a women-free work environment now or in the future. When female

employees know that a leave policy exists, their morale and productivity is higher.

2. *Recruitment*—A liberal policy would be a strong incentive for any person considering a job in the firm.

3. *Turnover*—No company can afford a high rate of turnover. The absence of a policy encourages young women to leave.

4. *Competition*—Many firms have these policies nowadays. If two companies are competing, the one without a policy is in a weakened position.

If your employer does not want to give you a lot of time, consider asking your employer to pay for your medical insurance coverage while on leave, or at least, to share the cost of keeping you on the company plan.

It takes time to initiate new company policies. You may not sell the idea the first time around, but if your argument is followed by others, in time your employer will have to reconsider. Feel proud of the fact that future working women will benefit from your efforts to make your job a better place to be.

Be aware that if your employer does not treat pregnancy as a disability, its policies probably do not conform to the Pregnancy Discrimination Act and applicable state law. In that case, you should consider contacting the federal Equal Opportunity Commission (or state's equivalent) or an attorney to explain what your rights are.

FYI: Does Maternity Leave Cost More?

A study by the Families and Work Institute, a nonprofit research group, finds that maternity leave costs a company less than it would cost to train a replacement. Other studies have shown that businesses that provide maternity leave profit in other ways: women are more loyal, more productive, miss fewer days at work, and work longer into their pregnancies. They are also more likely to return to the job after childbirth.

Work Options to Consider When Your Maternity Leave Ends

Now is the time to think about your working arrangements after you return from leave and to discuss the possibilities with your employer. Many alternatives are possible, although your particular job may not be adaptable to some of them. For example:

- *Return gradually*—This is a good option if you're breast-feeding. You might work fewer days a week or shorter hours each day and gradually increase your hours as your child-care responsibilities lessen.

- *Bring your baby to work*—This option may offer a temporary solution to your child-care problems if you cannot get an extension and have to go back to work full time and your boss finds you indispensable. You can do this if your workplace is somewhat private with a minimum of public contact. Because your infant will be sleeping most of the time, it shouldn't interfere with your work. The trick is to learn how to juggle those times when both your baby and your work need attention.

• *Leave of absence or sabbatical*—If you want to take off a much longer period of time but be assured you'll be able to come back to a job, inquire into these possibilities.

• *Trade-offs*—If your job requires much traveling, you may be able to trade with an associate until you're ready for full-time work. While your associate is on the road, you could be picking up the slack in the office.

• *Job sharing*—This method allows two people to share the duties of one job. It would work well with another mother, or perhaps a coworker who wants to start semi-retirement. It has advantages for working mothers and for employers who can then keep two valuable employees. Studies have shown that productivity rises under such circumstances, because each jobsharer produces more than 50 percent of the work, and that the turnover rate is lower. Benefits are shared too. To find someone to share with, ask the personnel department if they know of others. Try placements offices of nearby colleges and universities, or employment agencies. Or place an ad in the company or local newspaper.

• *Flextime or flexible scheduling*—You would still work a full job under this arrangement, but your hours would be at more convenient times. This means that the schedule changes from day-to-day or week-to-week, or it can mean that the hours are fixed but are not standard. It might permit you to share some of the child care with your partner or to work around your breast-feeding schedule. The drawback is that the rest of the world is still working nine to five. The array of flextime options include:

- *Flexihour:* Employee selects starting time.

- *Gliding schedule:* Within blocks of time, employee may vary hours without prior notifications or approval.

- *Variable time:* Employee must be present for a core time five days a week but may otherwise vary length of workday or workweek.

- *Maxiflex:* Similar to variable time, except that core time is scheduled on fewer days.

- *Compressed work week*—Full-time employees may work four ten-hour days a week; eight nine-hour days plus one eight-hour day over two weeks; or a week of five nine-hour days followed by a week of four nine-hour days with a day off every other week.

- *Voluntary reduced time*—V-time is an option that enables employees to reduce their pay and work time by 5 to 50 percent for a specified period—usually six to twelve months. Workers retain their benefits and seniority status on a prorated basis. Companies have begun offering this option to help employee's meet family, personal, or schooling needs, as well as offering it as an alternative to layoffs.

- *Telecommuting*—This allows you the comforts of home and a saving in expenses while communicating with your office through a computer, phone, and fax. You could vary your schedule as it suits you, working in the office some days or just going in for meetings. Regular weekly appearances are important to avoid "out of sight/out of mind," as well as the isolation factor. In many cases, telecommuters keep their benefits, salary, and advancement opportunities. Studies have shown that telecommuting increases productivity 20 to 60 percent and decreases turnover rate. You must set up a separate work area where nothing will be disturbed and have a caregiver for your baby. An answer machine on a separate business number or a business cell phone could take your calls when you are busy.

- *Part-time work*—(Sometimes called a "slightly shortened workday") Fewer than thirty-five hours per week, part-week or part-day. You and your employer would have to agree on your workload and who would handle the balance. Remember that your costs would be lower to balance the reduction in pay. You need to learn whether your benefits would continue under such an arrangement.

And you need to think about what effect it would have on your status at work. It might be better to find part-time work in another place. The drawbacks are that you would be working for an hourly wage and probably would not have benefits.

- *Trade-pay-for-time*—The next time you negotiate a pay raise, or are offered one at your performance review, acknowledge your employer's recognition of your performance and contribution to the company, then inform him that you'd like to trade your pay raise for time instead. For example, a 10 percent raise would be traded for four hours off each week. In some cases, you can negotiate more time than money (e.g., a 7 percent raise is traded for 10 percent time off).

- *Temporary work*—This might be an answer for an interim period.

- *Self-employment*—Freelancing or consulting offers you flexibility, but you must have flexible child care, too, because you never know when you're going to be working. A drop-in child-care center would be an advantage or a baby-sitter who's on call. Another advantage would be your freedom to do things, such as take your baby to the doctor.

Keep in mind that these elements can be combined: Flextime schedules can be full-time or part-time; part-time workers might also telecommute, and one job-share partner might work a compressed schedule to make physical room for the other partner. You can also propose a short-term, part-time schedule that only lasts two months. For more ideas, see "Options to Consider When Your Job and Motherhood Don't Mix," page 309.

SAMPLE MATERNITY LEAVE AGREEMENT

This agreement outlines the details of my maternity leave as agreed to in our meeting on _____ (date).

Length of Leave

Because my due date is _____, I plan to work full-time until _____ (unless otherwise advised by my doctor) at which time I will use weeks of vacation/sick time followed by ____ months leave of absence after the birth of my baby. After my leave, I will return to work on _____ to a (full-time, part-time, flexible) schedule until a change of schedule is agreed to.

Compensation and Benefits

I understand that I will be paid _____ percent of my salary the first _____ weeks of my leave, that is, _____ weeks of vacation/sick pay followed by _____ months of disability and _____ percent of my salary during weeks _____. I will receive my checks by mail every week. The remaining weeks of my leave of absence will be unpaid. My full benefits and profit-sharing participation will continue during the entire leave of absence.

Consultations

You have agreed to consult with me regarding the following clients/accounts:

_____

_____

_____

_____

_____

Work Arrangements

During my leave of absence, I propose that my work be handled by

_____.

I will train this person to ensure a smooth transition. My back-up will be

_____, who will fill in if necessary. (My part-time/flex-time, job-

sharing) agreement will include (details) _____

_____

_____.

The company will benefit from (details) _____

_____

_____.

Job Guarantee

Upon return to work on _____, I will come back to my current posi-

tion of _____.

Thank you,

Name _____Date_____

Approved by_____Date_____

FYI: Facts about Working Women

The number of women in the paid labor force has increased by 250 percent since the 1950s. In comparison, the labor force participation rate of men continues to decline.

- *Seven in ten working mothers work more than forty hours a week.*

- *Sixty-three percent of workers at or below the minimum wage were women in 2002.*

- *Women with children will account for over 75 percent of the growth in the American labor force by the year 2010.*

Our government and businesses need to act responsibly toward the American family. Meanwhile, we women need to continue to demand flexible work arrangements until employers develop new schedules: alternating work days, bigger blocks of time off, or satellite offices located near our homes in order to utilize our talent and prepare our country's greatest resource and future labor force—our children.

Chapter 9

Getting Ready for Baby on a Busy Schedule

If you are like most working women, you'll probably continue to work into your eighth month. Because there are so many details you'll need to take care of as you prepare for the new arrival, you'll want to make the most of your free time by being as organized and efficient as possible. Try to prepare as much as you can before your baby's birth—ideally by the end of the eighth month—in case you deliver early.

WORKING WOMAN'S NINE-MONTH CHECKLIST

To do within the first trimester (one to three months)

☐ Find an obstetrician, family physician, or midwife.

☐ Read some books about labor and delivery.

☐ Develop a birth plan.

☐ Tour and select a birth site.

☐ Make a list of important new telephone numbers to take to the office.

☐ Arrange your office or workspace for your comfort.

☐ Bring in the comfort supplies listed on page 21.

☐ Communicate with your boss or supervisor regarding on-the-job safety if necessary.

☐ Set up a budget.

☐ Make time to exercise.

To do within the second trimester (three to six months)

☐ Tell your boss and coworkers the news, unless you needed to do so earlier for any reason.

☐ Research your company's maternity/disability/insurance policies.

☐ Arrange your schedule to allow for exercise, comfort, and safety.

☐ Negotiate and make arrangements for your maternity leave at work.

☐ Shop for maternity clothes.

☐ Research and choose a childbirth class.

☐ Select a pediatrician.

☐ Decide on child-care options and reserve them.

☐ Get your nursery together (remodel, decorate, etc., with safety and comfort being your main consideration).

☐ Buy your baby supplies (especially a car seat for bringing your baby home from the hospital).

☐ Select and order your birth announcements.

☐ Stock up on nonperishable staples, including toiletries and baby-care supplies.

☐ Return library books, videotapes, and other borrowed items.

☐ Review your calendar for upcoming special occasions, such as birthdays and holidays.

☐ Buy cards and wrap gifts ahead of time.

☐ Arrange for any financial aid and medical support.

To do within your third trimester (six to nine months)

☐ Pick a few potential names for your baby.

☐ Cook and freeze a few meals, labeling them with contents, date of preparation, and heating instructions. Stock up on convenience foods.

☐ Pack your hospital bag.

☐ Buy a roll of stamps and several packages of thank-you notes.

☐ Continue to discuss your labor arrangements with your birth attendant.

☐ Put your bills, receipts, and other paperwork in order. Prepay some bills if you can.

☐ Pamper yourself with an easy-to-manage haircut, relaxing facial, or pretty manicure that you won't have time for later.

☐ Buy something you'll feel good about wearing after you have the baby.

☐ Visit your dentist for a checkup and cleaning, and make an appointment for X-rays after you have the baby.

☐ Set up a plan for sharing household and child-care responsibilities with your partner. Consider hiring help for tasks like housecleaning, lawn care, and laundry. Evaluate and streamline your home-care routine, eliminating unnecessary tasks and performing others less often but more efficiently.

☐ Plan for your work departure. Organize your workplace. Don't take any new work assignments. Tie together loose ends of any old projects.

☐ Find a pharmacy that offers delivery or drive-through service. Stock up on a two-month supply of whatever drugs and vitamins you'll need.

☐ Send thank-you cards for gifts.

☐ Take an infant Cardiopulmonary Resuscitation (CPR) class.

☐ Baby-proof your home.

After birth

☐ Send birth announcements.

☐ Make a postnatal appointment for you and your baby.

☐ Buy a diaper bag with several compartments and keep it stocked with: blanket, extra outfits, diapers, wipes, ointment, snacks for you, and feeding supplies.

☐ Place containers filled with diapers, wipes, and ointment around your house. You won't want to walk to the nursery every time your newborn needs to be changed.

☐ Have a baby memory book, a baby how-to book, and a notebook ready and accessible. You can fill them out whenever you have a spare minute.

☐ Develop a feeding "system." If nursing, have a small bag filled with the essentials: small pillow, blanket, bottle of water, and a cloth, which you can grab at a moment's notice when your baby is hungry.

☐ Make lists. It only takes a moment to jot down errands to run, items to buy, and things to do. The next time someone offers to help, you'll know exactly what needs to be done (and maybe if they see the list, they'll help even more).

BABY CARE CHECKLIST

Diaper-Changing and Grooming Supplies

☐ Cloth diapers and/or disposable diapers—Three or four dozen cloth diapers per week or two dozen if you also use a diaper service or combine with disposables; eighty to one hundred disposable diapers per week

☐ Four to five diaper covers or rubber pants—Use with cotton diapers

☐ Diaper liners for cloth and disposable diapers—Keeps baby dry throughout the night

☐ Four to six safety diaper pins (with double-locking heads) or clips, or masking tape—Closes a cloth, or recloses a disposable diaper

☐ Baby wipes—Use alcohol-free, fragrance-free ones with aloe or lanolin, and hypoallergenic ones, or washcloths or toilet paper (wipe warmers are optional)

☐ Cotton diapers—Catch baby's spit-ups during sleeping or feeding and to protect your clothing

☐ Petroleum jelly, diaper-rash ointments

☐ Baby powder

☐ Baby lotion or oil for dry or flaky skin

☐ Brush and comb

☐ Baby scale (optional)

☐ Small, blunt-tipped nail scissors or baby clippers

☐ Nursing and formula equipment—Bottles, nipples, nursing pillow, nursing pads, breast pump, etc.

☐ Cotton swabs or balls to clean ears and umbilical-cord stump

☐ Several terry-cloth wash cloths and/or a natural sponge

☐ Several soft, hooded bath towels large enough to wrap around baby

☐ Soap dish or a jar filled with a mild, pure soap

☐ Mild shampoo (after the first couple of months)

☐ Large towel or bath apron—To protect your clothes while bathing baby

☐ Plastic mat—For splashes in car or under high chair at home

First-Aid Supplies

☐ Rubbing alcohol—Helps to clean umbilical cord stump

☐ Sterile gauze pads and cloth adhesive tape—Protects the penis if baby has been circumcised or for minor injuries

☐ Infant liquid acetaminophen or fever-reducing medication (consult with your doctor before use)

☐ Thermometers (rectal and/or digital type)

☐ Syrup of Ipecac—Induces vomiting in certain cases of poisoning

☐ Antiseptic cream—Helps prevent infection of minor scrapes and cuts

☐ Tweezers—Removes splinters

☐ Lotions—Treat insect bits, poison ivy, etc.

☐ Eye wash

☐ Diarrhea fluid solution—Replaces lost electrolytes due to diarrhea

☐ Sunscreen

☐ Hydrogen peroxide—Cleanses abrasions and cuts

☐ Ice pack—Helps reduce swelling of bruises

☐ Teething gel

☐ Nasal aspirator (a rubber ball syringe with a two-inch bulb)

☐ Infant nose drops

☐ Humidifier (cool mist) or vaporizer (warm steam)—Helps relieve nasal and chest congestion, coughs, parched throats, and discomfort of colds and respiratory ailments (Change the water daily and clean according to manufacturer's instructions. Use distilled, not hard water. Get one with an automatic safety shutoff.)

Layette Supplies

☐ Sleepwear—Six to eight nightgowns, kimonos, or sleeping bags

☐ Shirts—Six to eight cotton short- or long-sleeved pull-ons with adjustable necks, or side-snap styles with opening at the front

☐ Stretch suits/onesies—Four one-piece suits with snap front for easy diaper changing

☐ Sweaters/snowsuits—One to two for cold weather (remember, they are outgrown quickly)

☐ Bunting—Warm blanket sacque with buttons or zipper for use in cold weather with a crotch for seat-belt fastening

☐ Hat/bonnet—One cotton or synthetic for summer, one knit for winter

☐ Socks/booties—Three to four pairs for cold outdoors or cool house

☐ Mittens

☐ Bibs—Four to six cotton or plastic to keep baby from getting wet and dirty during feeding

☐ Burping towels—Six to eight cotton towels to be worn over your shoulder while feeding and burping, or stretched across crib to catch any spit-ups

☐ Waterproof diaper covers—Four to five pairs of small plastic or treated cotton pants used with cotton diapers

BABY EQUIPMENT CHECKLIST

Description	Purchased from	Cost	Borrowed from
Baby safety equipment			
Bassinet/cradle			
Bathtub			
Bedding			
Booster chair			
Carrier			
Car seat			
Changing table			
Clothes hamper			
Crib/mattress			
Diaper bag			
Diaper pail			
Dresser			
Feeding equipment			
High chair			
Humidifier/vaporizer			
Monitor			
Playpen			
Rocking chair			
Stroller			
Swing			
Toy chest			

Description	Purchased from	Cost	Borrowed from
Walker			
Other			
Other			
Other			
Other			
Other			
Other			
Other			
Other			

WORKING WOMAN'S NINE-MONTH PLANNING CALENDAR

Your pregnancy will last an average of two-hundred-and-eighty days, forty weeks, or a little less than ten months. It starts from the first day of your last normal menstrual period. At your first prenatal visit, your health-care professional will help you determine an expected delivery date (EDD). If you deliver on your EDD, your baby will actually be only twenty-eight weeks old—that's because your egg didn't become fertilized until about two weeks after the start of your last menstrual period. It's important to remember that your due date is only an estimate—most babies are born between thirty-eight and forty-two weeks and only a small percentage of women actually deliver on their due date.

Use this monthly calendar to help you keep track of medical appointments, childbirth classes, and all your other monthly activities. You can also record your progress, your baby's vital stats, interesting observations, and special milestones. This calendar will not only help you manage your pregnancy more efficiently, it will become a wonderful memento after your baby is born.

MONTH _____

At one month your baby is half the size of the end of your little finger.

SUNDAY	MONDAY	TUESDAY	WEDNESDAY	THURSDAY	FRIDAY	SATURDAY

Notes:

_____

_____

_____

_____

_____

_____

_____

_____

_____

_____

_____

_____

_____

_____

_____

Pregnancy, from conception to birth, lasts approximately 22,896,000 seconds.

MONTH _____

At two months your baby is as large as the end of your thumb.

SUNDAY	MONDAY	TUESDAY	WEDNESDAY	THURSDAY	FRIDAY	SATURDAY

Notes:

_____

_____

_____

_____

_____

_____

_____

_____

_____

_____

_____

_____

_____

Babies born with the new moon will be eloquent speakers; those who arrive during the last quarter will be good reasoners.

MONTH _____

At three months your baby is the size of your entire thumb.

SUNDAY	MONDAY	TUESDAY	WEDNESDAY	THURSDAY	FRIDAY	SATURDAY

Notes:

_____

_____

_____

_____

_____

_____

_____

_____

_____

_____

_____

_____

_____

In the Carolinas, it is said that a baby born on the twenty-sixth of any month will become very, very rich.

MONTH _____

At four months your baby is about the size of a hot dog.

SUNDAY	MONDAY	TUESDAY	WEDNESDAY	THURSDAY	FRIDAY	SATURDAY

Notes:

_____
_____
_____
_____
_____
_____
_____
_____
_____
_____
_____
_____
_____
_____
_____

In the Middle East, a child born with a birthmark on the sole of the foot will grow up having a strong character.

MONTH _____

At five months your baby weighs a little under a pound and is 10 inches long.

SUNDAY	MONDAY	TUESDAY	WEDNESDAY	THURSDAY	FRIDAY	SATURDAY

Notes:

_____

_____

_____

_____

_____

_____

_____

_____

_____

_____

_____

_____

_____

An American superstition says that older parents bear more intelligent children.

MONTH _____

At six months your baby weighs about 1 1/2 pounds and is a little over 12 inches long.

SUNDAY	MONDAY	TUESDAY	WEDNESDAY	THURSDAY	FRIDAY	SATURDAY

Notes:

_____

_____

_____

_____

_____

_____

_____

_____

_____

_____

_____

_____

_____

A navel that sticks out is a sign of luck in life.

MONTH _____

At seven months your baby weighs 2 1/2 pounds and is 15 inches long.

SUNDAY	MONDAY	TUESDAY	WEDNESDAY	THURSDAY	FRIDAY	SATURDAY

Notes:

_____

_____

_____

_____

_____

_____

_____

_____

_____

_____

_____

_____

_____

Children born with hairy arms are headed for a prosperous life.

MONTH _____

At eight months your baby weighs 4 to 5 pounds and is 16 to 17 inches long.

SUNDAY	MONDAY	TUESDAY	WEDNESDAY	THURSDAY	FRIDAY	SATURDAY

Notes:

_____

_____

_____

_____

_____

_____

_____

_____

_____

_____

_____

_____

_____

Babies born with open hands will be generous.

MONTH _____

At nine months your baby weighs about 7 pounds and is 21 inches long—Congratulations!

SUNDAY	MONDAY	TUESDAY	WEDNESDAY	THURSDAY	FRIDAY	SATURDAY

Notes:

_____

_____

_____

_____

_____

_____

_____

_____

_____

_____

_____

_____

_____

Bald-headed babies are destined to be bright students.

Chapter 10

Time-Saving Ways to Find a Quality Baby Doctor

It's easier these days for a working mother to guarantee her child the best, healthiest start in life. Many physicians are changing their practices to accommodate women who work. According to the American Academy of Pediatrics, 60 percent of their members now offer regular weekend office hours and 50 percent have evening hours. Some baby-care doctors are even scheduling before-work appointments, installing twenty-four-hour emergency phone numbers, and accepting calls from child-care providers rather than from a parent.

Your choice of a baby doctor will depend on many factors, including convenient office location and cost.

Here are your most common options:

Pediatrician

These doctors specialize in the diseases and care of newborns, infants, children, and teenagers exclusively. Pediatricians are physicians who have selected a specialty and have passed the requirements of the American

Board of Specialties, generally after three years of additional training. Some pediatricians may also have additional training in subspecialties like neonatal care, child cardiology, or other special problems.

Family Physician
These doctors have had three years of residency in family practice medicine. They may be affiliated with a hospital, but not necessarily. Because their practices cover the care of people of all ages, they may not keep up with the latest techniques for treating complicated illnesses in newborns or young children.

General Practitioner
After medical school, these doctors have not had additional training in a specialty, and they may not be familiar with the latest techniques. Their fees are lower, however.

Pediatric Nurse-Practitioner
These professionals are registered nurses with advanced degrees in the care of infants and young children. They are trained to diagnose and treat common childhood diseases, give inoculations, and provide well-baby care, often at costs lower than that of a pediatrician. More serious disease requires the care of a physician. Like a physician's assistance, most nurse-practitioners work under the auspices of a pediatrician.

Well-Baby Clinic
These facilities charge only what the family is able to pay. They're usually

associated with a teaching or children's hospital, or a community service program. Care may be provided by a physician or a medical student, a nurse-practitioner, or other physician's assistant. Call your city, county or state health department for information on well-baby clinics in your area.

Conducting Initial Interviews by Telephone from Work

It's wise to begin your search for a doctor around the end of your second trimester. When you pick a doctor in advance, your baby will have continuity of care from the beginning. Some women run into the problem of finding a doctor who's just right but who doesn't have privileges at her preferred hospital. The decision then becomes whether to find another doctor or to use a hospital-selected pediatrician for your hospital stay.

• Ask coworkers, family, neighbors, school personnel, and friends whether they could recommend a doctor who's competent and gentle with children. Or turn to your family doctor or obstetrician for a referral to someone with a good reputation among peers. If that doesn't work, try the following resources:

• Nursing staff in the pediatric department of your hospital. Nurses see firsthand how well doctors interact with mothers and babies.

• County medical society

• Local major teaching hospital

- Director of medical specialists in the local library

- Before you make your calls, have a clear idea of your positions on issues of child health care, such as vaccines, alternative therapies, when to start solid food, and when to wean your child, so you will be able to discuss them intelligently. Because the field of pediatrics is usually in the process of change, your opinions may be just as valid as a pediatrician's.

- Let competence, compassion, and confidence be your guide. You want someone who not only can zero in on medical problems quickly, but who will be concerned with your baby's total emotional and physical picture. This person should also be supportive of your dual working/parenting roles.

- Choose up to four of the referrals you've gathered and start phoning during your lunch hour. Many of the questions you asked potential birth attendants about training, length of practice, hospital affiliation, and costs may also be used for a pediatrician interview, so go back and reread the relevant sections.

- When you've found someone who sounds concerned, flexible, and considerate, make an appointment for further discussion. As kids get older, they tend to prefer doctors who are of their same sex, so you may want to pick a female or a male doctor. Making sure you have the right person is worth the possible extra cost.

CRITICAL QUESTIONS FOR AN IN-PERSON INTERVIEW

A pediatrician's interview usually takes fifteen to thirty minutes (excluding the average wait time of a half hour). Remember to save time by calling ahead to ask if the doctor is running late. Also remember to seek advice from others in the waiting room, especially about the average time they wait. You can learn a lot about a practice by the way other parents feel about the doctor, and you will get a firsthand view of how the staff handles you and your child.

Note whether the waiting room is well equipped with toys and books to keep a child entertained. Bring *The Working Woman's Baby Planner* to ensure that you've asked the ten following relevant questions:

1. What is your medical education, training, and certification?

Feel free to call the schools to confirm or the State Medical Board to see if he's licensed. Ask questions to make sure the pediatrician is keeping up with current recommendations in pediatric medicine. A good resource for comparisons is the American Academy of Pediatrics. Another way to check out your doctor is to call the local medical society and ask for the public record of complaints on citations for your physician. Or call your local county civil records office to find out what your doctor's malpractice record looks like. You can also check with the Federation of State Medical Boards to see if there has been any serious disciplinary action, or professional peer reviews against the pediatrician. You can also get consumer advocate books from the Director of Public Citizen's Health Research Group that keeps track of doctors who have been disciplined by a state or the federal government. Get a copy of the list of *Books of Questionable Doctors,* organized by state.

2. Why did you choose pediatrics?

Open-ended questions like this will reveal much about the physician's personality and attitudes. Can you ask a silly question or does the doctor intimidate you? She shouldn't be impatient or condescending with you either.

3. How do you feel about working mothers?

It's crucial to find a doctor who respects your personal goals and your financial situation. If you detect an attitude disapproving of the way you live, it's time to move on. A pediatrician who supports working mothers will be more apt to accommodate to your work schedule and make it easier for you to call from work when you need advice. She or he will also avoid saying things that add to all your other anxieties.

4. Will you examine my newborn infant in the hospital? How often?

5. Where do you stand on the issue of _____?

You should also raise some of your values and your philosophy of mothering for discussion. Choose subjects that are important to you, such as:

• Placing a six-week-old in child care
• Allowing your baby to sleep in your bed
• Circumcising
• Feeding on demand

- Starting to feed solid food
- Bonding immediately after birth
- Pacifier/thumb-sucking
- Phone management of childhood illnesses

You should expect to receive literature regarding nutrition, development, and safety, as well as information about classes and other child-related activities.

6. Do you have call-in hours? What are your office hours? When are you available? Who will be answering questions?

Often a busy pediatrician will have a medical assistant or nurse practitioner take care of the common, nonurgent problems. Some offices actually have a 24/7 nurse's line just for this purpose. Are you or a backup doctor available twenty-four hours a day, seven days a week?

7. Do you separate well-baby and sick-baby appointments? What is your policy on medication? Do you prefer trying noninvasive aids first?

8. How do you handle emergencies?

The answer will tell you about hospital affiliations and what procedures to follow in the case of your child's illness. It should include directions about who to call after office hours. Do you make house calls? Under what circumstances?

9. What do you charge for office visits, lab tests, and immunizations?

Ask whether you will be charged for telephone consultations or a canceled appointment. Will you be billed for a visit or will you have to pay at once? Will they accept a credit card or a check? If a medical procedure is expensive, will you be able to pay in installments?

10. Does your staff do the paperwork or must I?

Once you've narrowed your decision to two contenders, trust your instincts to pick your baby's health-care provider you can trust and with whom you can talk openly. You won't want to feel as if she or he can't talk at your level, and you don't want to feel as if the doctor is too busy to answer your question. You want a pediatrician who you respect, who will meet all your needs, and who will be available for the long-term as your child grows.

Questionable Care

Discomfort with medical care and a doctor's ability to make quality referrals is unsettling. If you don't trust your pediatrician, you may need to consult another doctor. But if medical wrongdoing is involved, it may be time to take stronger action.

If you sense something is wrong, go with your instincts. Remove your child from the doctor's care immediately. Secondly, address any medical problems. Call your state health department to discuss what has happened. Thirdly, if you suspect wrongdoing, look into legal recourse. Many malpractice suits could be avoided with good communication. Ask lots of questions and understand what procedures are being performed and why.

If you end up switching doctors, make sure to get a copy of your child's medical records for your next physician. Courts have recognized that while physical records are the property of a physician, consumers have a right to the information in those records. In most states, doctors are bound by statute to turn over a copy of records—copy fees may be charged. For quick action, have your new physician make the request. Also, you can contact your state consumer pediatrician bureau or an attorney.

PEDIATRICIAN ESTIMATE WORKSHEET

	Description of Services	Costs
1. Name _____	_____	_____
Address_____	_____	_____
City_____	_____	_____
Phone_____	_____	_____
Nurse _____	_____	_____
Ref'd by _____	_____	_____
Comments_____	_____	_____
_____	_____	_____
_____	_____	_____
_____	_____	_____
_____	_____	_____
2. Name _____	_____	_____
Address_____	_____	_____
City_____	_____	_____
Phone_____	_____	_____
Nurse _____	_____	_____
Ref'd by _____	_____	_____
Comments_____	_____	_____
_____	_____	_____

	Description of Services	Costs
_____	_____	_____
_____	_____	_____
_____	_____	_____
_____	_____	_____

3. Name _____ _____ _____

Address_____ _____ _____

City_____ _____ _____

Phone_____ _____ _____

Nurse _____ _____ _____

Ref'd by _____ _____ _____

Comments_____ _____ _____

_____ _____ _____

_____ _____ _____

_____ _____ _____

_____ _____ _____

Name of Selected Pediatrician_____

Address_____

City_____Zip _____

Phone _____Emergency Phone _____

Hours _____

Total Cost _____Extra costs _____

Notes:_____

Preparing for the Hospital Ahead of Time

Find out in advance the items the hospital supplies and those you must provide. A hospital staff member or your childbirth educator should have the answers. Then make these preparations:

- Start packing a small suitcase for the hospital after your eighth month. Keep a second suitcase at work or carry one in the car. Use the checklist provided to help you remember everything. Leave jewelry and other valuables at home.

- Keep at least a quarter tank of gas in your car at all times.

- Keep a phone card and money for tolls in your car.

- Keep the phone number of a twenty-four-hour taxi service at your desk, and at home, just in case.

- Rehearse your route to the hospital and an alternate in case of traffic problems with your designated driver. Get a sense of the timing, especially at lunch hour and rush hour when traffic may be heavy.

- Know which hospital door to enter and what route to take to the maternity area. When childbirth is imminent, you don't want to be wandering around lost in a big hospital.

HOSPITAL SUITCASE CHECKLIST

Your Suitcase

☐ Two or three nightgowns, with or without access for nursing

☐ One bathrobe

☐ Slippers, socks, or sandals (for the shower, too)

☐ Two or three tight bras if you're not nursing, or two or three comfortably fitting nursing bras that you purchased at the end of your eighth month

☐ Eyeglasses and contacts (contacts may not be allowed during labor)

☐ Tape/CD player

☐ One box of breast pads

☐ Four or five underpants (maternity or regular)

☐ Sanitary napkins

☐ Toothbrush and toothpaste

☐ Massage oil or lotion

☐ Comb, brush, and small mirror

☐ Makeup and toiletries

☐ Hair ties or barrettes

☐ Birth announcements, pen, and mailing list

☐ Telephone book and phone numbers (maybe even a long-distance calling card)

☐ Reading material

☐ Sweets to suck on during labor if your doctor approves them; mints to keep your mouth fresh

☐ Family photos

- [ ] Loose-fitting going-home clothes
- [ ] Lip balm or petroleum jelly for dry lips
- [ ] Any special medications or vitamins that you may be taking

Labor Coach or Partner's Suitcase

- [ ] Stopwatch to time contractions
- [ ] Camera with flash, film, and /or video camera with tape
- [ ] Tennis ball or rolling pin to help with back labor
- [ ] Radio, cassette player, and tapes for relaxation
- [ ] Stuffed animal or picture to help focus your concentration
- [ ] Healthful snack food for quick energy (your coach's energy!)
- [ ] Insurance paperwork and completed registration forms
- [ ] Natural sponge to wipe your face
- [ ] Pillows and pillowcases (hospitals sometimes use uncomfortably hot, plastic-covered ones)
- [ ] Relaxation materials like books, music, candles, magazines, etc.

Baby's bag

- [ ] Two fancy outfits for picture-taking and going home
- [ ] One warm hat or bonnet
- [ ] One blanket or bunting with a crotch for seat-belt fastening
- [ ] Socks or booties
- [ ] Car seat—Most hospitals rent car seats in case you don't have one

What to Do If Labor Starts at Work

Most first labors last for many hours so there shouldn't be an immediate need for you to rush off to the hospital. Call your spouse and/or labor coach to pick you up from work and take you home where you'll be more comfortable while laboring. If you're not feeling well, find a quiet, private place to rest while a trusted coworker makes the call, informs your boss/supervisor about your situation, and perhaps even stays with you until your ride arrives. Of course, if you are beginning to deliver, or feel that you're experiencing a medical emergency (sudden bleeding, faintness, or excruciating pain), you should call your doctor, 911, or a private ambulance service immediately.

In the early stages of labor, contractions will last about thirty seconds, building up to ninety seconds or even longer at the end of the first stage. You may also feel the following:

- *Your baby dropping*—As your baby moves downward and forward, your abdominal pressure will lessen and breathing will be easier. This is called "dropping" or "lightening." It may occur at any time in the last four weeks but usually doesn't happen until labor starts. Now the pressure will be on your bladder. You can expect frequent urination, shooting pains down your legs, and an increase in vaginal discharge.

- *False contractions*—Short, irregular spasms, called Braxton-Hicks contractions, may occur in late pregnancy. They may be stopped with a change of activity; for example, shifting from standing to sitting down.

Because the best way to keep your mind off these false contractions is to keep busy, the working woman has an advantage. Try not to worry unduly or let nervousness drive you to the hospital prematurely.

- *Premenstrual-like symptoms*—Cramps, pressure on your rectum, and wanting to empty your bladder and bowels are early signs that labor is about to begin.

How to Recognize True Labor: Questions and Answers

1. *Your "bag of waters" breaks*—The bag of amniotic fluid that cradles your baby may rupture at any time during labor. It might be small dribbles of fluid or a sudden flood. Don't confuse this with small gushes of urine when you sneeze or cough.

   What should you do?
   Use a sanitary napkin (keep one handy at work and in your car) to catch the flow, and call your doctor, birth attendant, and/or labor coach. Alert your doctor, birth attendant, and/or labor coach that you're ready to go to the hospital because there is always a risk of infection even when contractions are not present.

2. *A "show" appears*—Either before or during labor, you'll pass a plug of thick, blood-stained mucus. Labor pains may begin within forty-eight to seventy-two hours after its appearance.

What should you do?

Wait until regularly spaced pains begin in your abdomen or back (indicating a back labor), or your water breaks, before calling your doctor or midwife.

3. *Regular contractions begin*—Labor pains feel like persistent bad menstrual cramps, a dull backache, or shooting pains in your legs. They should be stronger and more frequent as time passes and each one should last for at least forty-five seconds.

What should you do?

Ask a nearby coworker to help you time regular contractions (once every fifteen to twenty minutes) jotting down the time each one begins and ends. Follow your physician's directions for when to call him or her—probably when your contractions are ten minutes apart and last forty seconds or more. If you won't have time to go home first, or have your designated driver meet you at work because you're actively in labor, notify your boss that your labor has begun, and ask a close coworker to drive you directly to the hospital.

Strategies for Relieving Labor Discomfort on the Job

Depending on how much privacy you have, use the following techniques to help you stay relaxed until it's time to leave for the hospital:

• Kneel with your legs apart, upper body relaxing against pillows or a pile of newspapers. You want your baby to move down so keep your torso upright as much as possible. Relax to a sitting position between contractions. If you find it necessary to lie down, lie on your side, not your back, with pillows supporting your head and upper thighs.

- Place one cushion on the seat of a chair and another against the back while you sit facing the back of the chair, resting your head on your arms.

- Urinate often to reduce the pressure on your uterus and your bladder.

- Walking the aisles and corridors of your building will strengthen the contractions and speed up a sluggish labor.

- During a contraction, look at a fixed spot, or recite a poem, or say a prayer if you're so inclined, to take your mind off yourself. Concentrate on getting through one contraction at a time.

- Breathe deeply and evenly at the beginning of a contraction and at the end, inhaling through your nostrils and exhaling through your mouth maintaining a steady rhythm. Limit shallow breathing to avoid dizziness.

- If the contractions are accompanied by a strong urge to push, it's a sign that the second stage of labor is beginning. Or, you may feel as if you have to have a bowel movement. Call for your designated driver to get your hospital bag and leave for the hospital as soon as possible. In the meantime, during a contraction, take two short inhalations followed by one long exhalation; that is, say, "ha, ha, blow." Then kneel down, lean forward, rest your head in your arms, and stick your bottom in the air. This will make pushing more difficult and reduce the urge. Breathe out slowly when it fades.

- Avoid food and drink during labor to reduce the chances of vomiting. If you must have something, stick to light, easily digested carbohydrate foods, such as bread, fruit, rice and pasta; and light protein foods, such as cheese and yogurt.

- Overcome nausea between contractions with small sips of cool water, or slowly eat dry toast and crackers. Keep frozen cranberry or grape juice in the office refrigerator. Crushed ice made from these juices or plain ice helps to ward off nausea.

Chapter 11

Budget Strategies to Meet Your Family's Growing Needs

Once a new baby is expected, parents begin thinking in new ways about the use of money, and above all, about the welfare of the family. Where you were once carefree and impulsive, now you'll begin to think for the long term about the steps you'll need to take to secure your child's future.

Strategies for Financial Security

Investigate the following areas; you will want to cover most, if not all of them for the protection of your new family:

1. *Maintain adequate medical coverage*—Most employers offer health insurance coverage only while the individual is employed at that company. A change of job means a change in insurance coverage, and nowadays, that often means that preexisting, chronic medical problems will not be covered by the new insurer. It might be wise to keep

your options open if a job change is in your future. Buy your own individual policy to cover chronic conditions and consider keeping the costs low with a high deductible.

2. *Prepare for short-term disability*—Any disability means that physical problems interfere with your ability to perform your duties at work. A pregnancy-related disability may fall under one of the following categories:

• *Side effects*—Some women suffer side effects, such as nausea, vomiting, indigestion, dizziness, or swollen limbs, which are considered disabilities.

• *Complications*—Serious complications, such as infections, bleeding, or early rupture of the amniotic sac, are considered disabilities. Chronic conditions, such as heart disease, diabetes, or high blood pressure, may worsen during pregnancy.

• *Job-related*—Such factors as exposure to high levels of toxic substances may cause disability.

If your doctor decides that your problem is disabling, you may request a letter verifying to your employer that you're eligible for disability benefits. (Your employer, on the other hand, may request a letter from the doctor confirming that you are, in fact, able to keep working.) To apply for disability benefits, contact your state Employment Development Department.

3. *Prepare for long-term disability*—The government mandates that employers provide short-term disability insurance that covers your salary for up to six weeks. They are not required to cover long-term disability, perhaps the most important consideration for parents with dependent children (see "Disability Insurance," page 209).

4. *Sign Power of Attorney agreements*—Both parents should negotiate Power of Attorney agreements appointing each other to handle finances in the event of an emergency.

5. *Write a "Living Will"*—Despite its name, a Living Will has nothing to do with inheritance. It provides protection, nevertheless, against a family having to make life-or-death decisions for one incapacitated member. While you're healthy, you sign this document stating your choices in the event you become unable to make your own decisions. Some states have a similar document, called a Durable Power of Attorney for health care, in which you appoint someone to make your medical decisions and state your choices if you desire.

6. *Draw up a Will*—A Will provides for the distribution of your estate according to your desires. Perhaps more important for parents, a Will can appoint a guardian for your children, and a trustee to take care of

his/her finances. Without a Will, the state will make those decisions.

7. *Start an emergency fund*—Every family should have an accessible emergency fund containing the equivalent of three months' income. A self-employed person, or one with a shaky job future, should have a fund equaling six months' income.

8. *Reduce your debt*—Pay off all your debts, especially high-interest credit card bills. The incentive is even greater now that consumer interest is not tax-deductible. Comparison shop for insurance plans. You could save a lot of money per year.

9. *Establish an emergency credit line*—Most banks offer these credit lines, which you can draw upon when needed. Interest is charged only when you've taken a loan. Also consider a home equity loan. It has the added advantage of tax deductibility.

10. *Lower your housing costs*—Mortgage interest rates have been lower in recent years than most can remember. Experts expect them to stay low for the foreseeable future. That means now is the time to refinance. If you can reduce your rate by at least two percentage points and expect to stay in your home for at least five years, it'll be worth your while. Comparison shop your utilities as well. While you may not be able to change who provides your water and electricity, there are certainly many phone companies and Internet providers looking for your business.

11. *Maintain adequate life insurance*—Your coverage should be approximately two to three times your family's annual gross income. Be sure you carry an individual policy that covers the difference between what you need and what your employer covers.

12. *Update the beneficiaries of retirement accounts like IRAs and 401(k)s to reflect your current intentions*—Even if you won't be naming your child as the primary beneficiary, naming a child as a contingent beneficiary could have great tax advantages later on.

Determining the Costs of Having a Baby

The arrival of a baby brings about important changes in a family's financial picture. Obviously, you'll have the immediate expenses for clothes, equipment, and in most cases, child-care expenses. Then there are the long-term considerations: Housing and insurance changes, perhaps; tax strategies; education costs; and inheritance decisions, among others. Chances are you will still spend 15–20 percent of your income on child-related expenses.

The smartest step you can take is to compare your current expenses and income with anticipated expenses and income and consider the budget you'll need to accomplish your objectives. The charts provided on pages 195–199 will help you get started.

If the money remaining at the end of the month is zero or a negative number:

1. Review your monthly expenses to see what can be reduced, modified, or eliminated.

2. Consult with a financial planner who can lay out a twelve-month budget.

3. Study budgeting books.

4. Investigate other sources of monthly income.

Evaluate your insurance coverage and plan for your maternity costs by using the checklist provided on the next page.

CHILDBIRTH COSTS WORKSHEET

	Item Covered Yes/No	Initial Cost	Insurance Payment	Actual Cost
Services				
Doctor's fees	☐ ☐	_____	_____	_____
Prenatal visits	☐ ☐	_____	_____	_____
Vaginal delivery	☐ ☐	_____	_____	_____
Caesarean delivery	☐ ☐	_____	_____	_____
In-hospital visits	☐ ☐	_____	_____	_____
Phone consultations	☐ ☐	_____	_____	_____
Postpartum checkup	☐ ☐	_____	_____	_____
Anesthesiologist	☐ ☐	_____	_____	_____
Anesthesia	☐ ☐	_____	_____	_____
Consulting physicians (high-risk pregnancy)	☐ ☐	_____	_____	_____
Other	☐ ☐	_____	_____	_____
Hospital/Birth Center				
Special tests/procedures	☐ ☐	_____	_____	_____
Lab work	☐ ☐	_____	_____	_____
Genetic counseling	☐ ☐	_____	_____	_____
Testing	☐ ☐	_____	_____	_____
Classes	☐ ☐	_____	_____	_____
Prenatal	☐ ☐	_____	_____	_____
Breast-feeding	☐ ☐	_____	_____	_____

Baby care   ☐ ☐   _____ _____ _____

Other   ☐ ☐   _____ _____ _____

Medication

Prenatal vitamins   ☐ ☐   _____ _____ _____

Other   ☐ ☐   _____ _____ _____

Recovery Supplies

Pediatrician   ☐ ☐   _____ _____ _____

Newborn exam   ☐ ☐   _____ _____ _____

Well-baby visits   ☐ ☐   _____ _____ _____

Immunizations   ☐ ☐   _____ _____ _____

Sick-baby visits   ☐ ☐   _____ _____ _____

Nursery supplies   ☐ ☐   _____ _____ _____

Deduct initial cost from insurance payment to arrive at actual cost:

Initial Total: _____ Actual Total: _____

Policy's yearly deductible $ _____

Remaining Deductible $ _____

One-Time Expenses

Moving/Construction $ _____

Decorating $ _____

Baby proofing $ _____

Furniture $ _____

Baby Announcements $ _____

Total $ _____

BEFORE-AND-AFTER EXPENSES COMPARISON CHART

Monthly Fixed Expenses	Before	After
Food	_____	_____
Housing	_____	_____
Transportation	_____	_____
Insurance	_____	_____
Health	_____	_____
Disability	_____	_____
Life	_____	_____
Auto	_____	_____
Dental	_____	_____
Homeowners	_____	_____
Taxes	_____	_____
Property	_____	_____
Income	_____	_____
Social Security	_____	_____
Pocket Money	_____	_____
Other	_____	_____
Total	_____	_____

Monthly Variable Expenses	Before	After
Installment payments	_____	_____
Credit cards	_____	_____

Loans _____ _____
Other _____ _____
Utilities _____ _____
Water and power _____ _____
Electricity _____ _____
Telephone _____ _____

Monthly Variable Expenses **Before** **After**

Charitable donations _____ _____
Education _____ _____
Entertainment _____ _____
Fitness/beauty _____ _____
Recreation/vacation _____ _____
Gifts _____ _____
Repairs/service calls _____ _____
Dry cleaning _____ _____
Investments _____ _____
Retirement _____ _____
Savings accounts _____ _____
Mutual funds _____ _____
Other _____ _____
Total _____ _____

Monthly Added Expenses   **After**

Child care   _____

Equipment   _____

Clothing   _____

Maternity & baby   _____

Total   _____

Combined Monthly Income

Salary/wages   _____

Bonuses   _____

Interest/dividends   _____

Other   _____

Total   _____

Enter your total monthly income $ _____

Subtract your monthly expenses $ _____

Net income after expenses deduction $ _____

Customizing a Benefits Package to Meet Your Needs

At one time, all benefit packages looked alike. But once women began entering the workforce in numbers, many couples found themselves with double benefits in some areas and none in others. The answer to that problem has been flexible benefits.

Most employers nowadays allocate a certain amount of money for each employee, and the worker chooses from among the available benefits. Benefit options usually include health insurance; short-term disability insurance; and retirement plans. Dependent-care-assistance plans are now included in the choices. In some plans, the employees' contributions may be deducted before taxes. In others, additional vacation, sick, and personal days may be combined.

Once you've completed the charts on pages 195–199 and studied the options, you'll be able to determine where your financial structure needs strengthening. Then you can choose the benefit package that fits your family's needs.

Health Insurance

Any health insurance provided by an employer must cover expenses for pregnancy-related conditions on the same basis as costs for other medical conditions. Under a law known as HIPAA, the Health Insurance Portability and Accountability Act of 1996, health insurers cannot consider pregnancy a preexisting condition. So, unlike illnesses such as diabetes, they can't deny you coverage when you go from one job to another and switch health plans.

Under the Consolidated Omnibus Reconciliation Act (COBRA) you are allowed to continue on a health insurance plan for up to eighteen months after you leave a business (with twenty or more employees) so that preexisting health conditions, such as pregnancy, may be covered while you're not working. When your COBRA coverage period is over, however, you may qualify for guaranteed-issue individual coverage. Check with your state's Department of Insurance for more alternatives. For the specific limitation periods in your state, contact the Department of Insurance Consumers Affairs Division or equivalent office.

Comparing Health Insurance Policies
Coverage for health care is usually the most important benefit to consider. Find out first whether your plan or your spouse's plan gives you better benefits, like the option of substituting cash value for medical coverage. Then the cash from that policy can be used for other necessities while the second policy provides health coverage. That's important to note because employers must provide the same level of health benefits for spouses of males employees as they do for spouses of female employees, as well as for women who work for the company.

If you are thinking of keeping both policies for the additional coverage, be sure to understand your plan's "coordination of benefits" clause. In some cases, insurance companies don't allow duplicate coverage or agree to pick up coverage where another policy leaves off.

Most group plans cover obstetrician's fees and hospital charges in their basic protection plus major medical policies. For major medical coverage only, you'll pay a deductible and co-insurance (ranging from 20 to 80 percent) for these costs. The typical policy covers prenatal appointments, lab tests, and whatever your doctor thinks is medically necessary. Labor-room and hospital-room charges are usually covered. Some insurers, however, reserve the right to evaluate the appropriateness of certain procedures.

In addition, check on the following points:

• Prepregnancy planning visit with your health care provider

• Number of hospital days covered

• Prenatal tests

• Restrictions against preexisting conditions

• Lifetime benefit limit

• Physician and hospital selection

• Exclusions

• "Reasonable and customary" clause

• Paperwork responsibility

- Payment method

- Carryover of charges to next year's deductible

- Co-payment. If so, how much?

- Deductible. If so, how much?

- Sick and well-baby visits

- Nursery costs of baby

The following types of plans are generally available:

- *Blue Cross/Blue Shield*—Each state has a separate not-for-profit Blue Cross/Blue Shield plan, which varies in the details. Under these policies, you choose which doctor in private practice you want to attend you. Their individual policies are sometimes cheaper than others.

- *Health Maintenance Organization (HMO)*—These groups employ physicians and other health-care professionals. In general, you don't have a choice of who will treat you except among several doctors in one specialty. Look for convenient location, board-certified physicians, and low turnover. Some HMOs accept individuals as well as groups.

- *Preferred Provider Organizations (PPO)*—A combination of features from the preceding two, PPOs offer a network of participating private-practice doctors and hospitals at little, or no, extra cost. Unlike HMOs, they reimburse up to 80 percent of medical charges incurred outside of their plan. Look for annual deductible and cost limitations.

If you are about to change jobs, try and get your previous plan to cover the entire pregnancy and delivery before making the switch. If this means a much higher bill, see if your new job has a medical "flex" plan that you can use to pay the higher premium. If it is not possible to carry over your old insurance, investigate your new insurance options, and make sure they cover preexisting conditions.

If you find yourself without any health insurance during your pregnancy and leave of absence, check with your state's Department of Social Services or Department of Health Care Access to see if there are other options, such as Medicaid or low-cost insurance plans that might help. You could also work with your obstetrician's office to identify low-cost alternatives to private health insurance in your area, and talk to an insurance broker, who should have information on plans for which you might qualify.

Whether or not you have insurance, you will definitely want to find out how much you will need to pay out for prenatal care and the delivery. You will want to make payment arrangements with your doctor or midwife, as the federal government reports that unreimbursed medical bills for an OB and hospital alone can total thousands of dollars.

HEALTH INSURANCE QUESTIONS AND ANSWERS

You can save money, sometimes substantial amounts, by understanding the fine print in your policy. Take the time to study, for example, the criteria that must be met before the company will pay so that you can determine if the medical procedure undertaken qualifies as a covered expense. The following questions are often raised about health insurance policies:

1. *Does it matter whether I buy equipment or my physician orders it?* It certainly does. Insurers are fussy about that. For example, if your doctor orders a breast pump while you're in the hospital, the cost might be covered. If you buy one after you've left the hospital, it might not be covered.

2. *What can I do if certain items are not covered under my policy?* Ask your doctor or hospital whether those items or procedures are really necessary. If so, you may want to try to negotiate a lower price.

3. *Now that I am pregnant, should I increase my insurance coverage?* Sorry, you should have thought about that earlier. Supplementary insurance coverage is not an option once you're pregnant. That's what they mean by preexisting condition. Your best option is to rely on savings. Of course, if you already have pregnancy coverage, there may still be some things you'll have to pay for out of pocket. Read "Determining the Costs of Having a Baby," page 193, to know what your obligations will be.

4. *Do I need to notify my insurance company that I am expecting or to modify my policy once my baby has arrived?* Yes, ASAP! You need to know when you must officially "pre-certify" your baby to the policy as well as how much the premium will increase when you do. Some insurance companies have certain restrictions and requirements about notification. You may need to call when you arrive at the hospital to deliver; otherwise they won't cover you and/or your baby.

5. *What happens to my insurance if I lose my job or quit?* You should be aware that, under the law, you are protected by COBRA which entitles you to buy coverage in your former employer's group health insurance plan for eighteen months after you leave. After that, you may convert to an individual policy if the plan has a conversion option. Sad to say, not many do.

6. *What will happen if I don't pay my premium on time?* If you don't pay within the usual thirty-one day grace period, you'll lose your insurance coverage.

7. *Does it matter when I file a claim?* Most, if not all, policies have time limits for filing claims. Make sure you know what yours is. If you miss the deadline, you might not qualify for benefits.

8. *When should I review my policy?* It's a good idea to review your policy each time it renews to make sure your coverage is up to date, your benefits are keeping up with inflation, and your premium cost is competitive with other comparable polices.

Health Insurance Information

When you've made your decision about health insurance, keep the following information about your chosen policy:

Company Name
Effective Date
Policyholder's Name
Policy Number
Social Security Number
Plan Code
Benefits Code
Deductibles
Family
Individual
Mother
Baby

What to Do When Your Insurer Rejects a Medical Claim

Nowadays, insurers are increasingly rejecting legitimate medical claims because of soaring medical costs. But they don't always get away with it; persistent consumers can get them to reverse their decisions. The following suggestions will help you present a good case for reversal of a rejection:

- *Keep records*—Always keep copies of correspondence and notes from telephone calls. A documented case is more persuasive.

- *Pursue an explanation*—In many states, insurance companies are required to explain their reasons for rejection. You may find it in the "Explanation of Benefits" portion of your statement. If you don't find it, call the insurer's toll-free number and pursue it until you understand the reason. Request an answer in writing.

- *Talk to your doctor*—The problem may be a simple clerical error, such as a missing social security number, that can be easily remedied. If it's more complicated, discuss the case with your doctor. She or he may be your best ally and probably knows the tricks of the trade. If you submit a letter from your doctor, it may be the most effective tactic, especially if the procedure in question is experimental or unusual. If nothing works, try to negotiate a reduced fee for medical procedures that are not covered.

- *Write an appeal letter*—A rejection must be appealed in writing within sixty days for the rejection. Write the president of the firm; enclose copies of all your documentation, and perhaps a copy of the disputed section of the benefits book with your interpretation of it.

- *Keep writing*—Write again if the first appeal doesn't work. You may be able to negotiate a satisfactory payment. If all else fails, call the State Insurance Department number, usually found in the government section of the telephone book.

- *Take them to court*—Engage in legal action as a last resort, especially if your claim involves a large sum of money. Look for a lawyer who specializes in insurance bad faith claims and will take your case on a contingency basis (meaning your attorney only gets paid if and when you get paid).

FYI: Sources of Help for the Health Insurance Consumer

Two organizations have been formed to help you when you're having difficulty dealing with an insurance company. They are:

National Insurance Consumer Helpline (800) 942-4242

National Insurance Consumer Organization (703) 549-8050

Disability Insurance

It's very important that the income earner(s) have disability insurance to provide for the family if they are disabled and can't work. Although disability insurance is more expensive than life insurance, people between the ages of thirty-five and sixty-five are more likely to become disabled than to die. Some firms provide disability insurance coverage, although it may not be enough to cover your obligations as a parent. Adequate coverage would be about 60 to 70 percent of your current income.

You will pay income tax on any benefits you receive through coverage paid for by your employer. Benefits from an individual policy (where you pay the premium) are not considered income for tax purposes. This makes a difference when considering how much coverage you need.

If your employer doesn't provide this benefit, don't assume that state government insurance will meet your costs. You may have to buy private insurance to make up the difference. Shop around for the best coverage for your age, occupation, and sex. Disability policies are expensive, and it is important to read the fine print.

Some states permit those on family leave to obtain partial wage replacement through the Temporary Disability Insurance (TDI). TDFI is a state-administered program similar to the unemployment insurance program. It provides partial wage replacement to qualified employees who are temporarily unable to work because of an illness or injury. Ask your human resources representative whether some of your leave can be paid through this plan.

Unlike term life insurance, there are many variables among disability policies. Speak with the benefits provider at your work and be sure to understand the following:

- *Sick leave*—How many days are you entitled to and at what rate of pay? They may have changed over time with your length of service to the company.

- *Worker's Compensation*—If your disability results from a job-related injury, worker's compensation may provide some benefit. But don't look for it to replace your salary, especially if you are a high-end earner. States usually cap the benefit at two-thirds of the average statewide wage.

- *Long-term disability*—Only about 40 percent of workers in medium-size and large companies receive this coverage, and even fewer employees of small companies are protected. What's more, you may not qualify for coverage unless you've worked at the job for several years.

Unemployment Insurance

Ask your employer whether you can collect income under your state-administered Unemployment Insurance (UI) program. A Department of Labor regulation passed in 2000 permits states to allow employees on family leave to receive partial wage employment through the UI system. So far, no state has yet taken advantage of the change in law and offered a plan to do this, but by the time you need it, your state may have become the first to do so.

Homeowner's Liability Insurance

With a baby in your home, the number of visitors will probably increase. Also, you're responsible for the safety of your caregiver. Make sure your accident liability insurance coverage is adequate to cover the added risks.

Life Insurance

If you do not have a life insurance policy, you should consider purchasing one. This coverage becomes more crucial with dependent children in the family. When both parents are contributing to the family income, each one should be covered for the possibility that one parent, or both, might die young. Some employers offer this coverage; if not, you should consider buying your own policy. If you're already covered by a particular policy, you need to make sure it's adequate for your added responsibilities, or else see your insurance broker.

Whether you are purchasing insurance for the first time or modifying your present plan, compare the different plans available. Your criteria should include:

1. Amount of coverage
   - Number of children
   - Double or single-income family
   - Liquid assets

2. Types of insurance
   - Benefits your family the most (term, variable, whole life, etc.)
   - Provides you with equity
   - Allows you to borrow against it
   - Has a cash surrender value if policy is canceled
   - Has tax-deferred interest
   - Has tax-free death benefits

3. Premiums and interest rates
   - Cost monthly, quarterly, or yearly
   - Yearly increase in premium costs
   - Projected interest rate
   - Expense charges
   - Amount of policy value in five years, ten years, etc.

4. Medical checkups
   - Medical checkup required
   - Conditions that would result in increased premiums

5. Beneficiaries
   - Amount of beneficiaries that can be stipulated upon
   - Rules and regulations for naming a minor as beneficiary

Allow a few days to pass before you make a decision regarding purchasing any life insurance. Never buy so much insurance that you have trouble meeting your current expenses. Also, don't be talked into buying insurance for your child. Instead, add a rider to cover funeral expenses for any family member.

Taking Advantage of Tax Benefits

Although your expenses will increase with the arrival of a new baby, your child may also have important tax saving consequences for your family. Some of these include your personal exemptions and possibly the deductibility of medical costs, which are subject to certain limitations.

The federal government provides assistance programs through Dependent Care Assistance Plans that allow a taxpayer to use pretax dollars to pay their child-care expenses. Such an account could save you 20 percent or more on your child-care expenses by reducing your taxable income. Ask your personnel or human resources department if your company is participating. Or ask for a handbook explaining how a program is established from: Massachusetts Public Interest Research Group Education Fund, 44 Wintes St. 4th Floor, Boston, MA 02108, phone (617) 292-4800.

Don't delay investigating this option. You may have to sign up before the year in which you plan to use the account. In addition, certain tax savings may be obtained by claiming the Child-Care Credit, which reduces your tax obligations as a result of certain qualified child-care expenses. This credit may include expenses associated with the cost of the following:

- Wages of a caregiver, including social security taxes (or the cost of an approved child-care center).

- Worker's compensation insurance (purchased for your protection, as well as that of the caregiver, in case she is injured on the job).

- Transportation costs from home to day-care center (possibly to the doctor's office as well).

- Classes for learning disabilities.

- Child-care costs while you attend job-required classes.

Contact an accountant to explore the deductibility of these types of expenses within the context of your financial condition. Or call the Internal Revenue Service at (800) 829-1040.

Part Three

Finding and Maintaining First-Rate Child Care

Chapter 12

Evaluating Your Child-Care Options

One of the first decisions you must make regarding child care is what type will best meet your needs and those of your child. Child care in the United States falls into three categories: in-home care, family day care, and center care. Each has its own advantages and disadvantages.

New working parents generally prefer home care for their babies at least until the babies are a couple of years old. Most people believe that individual attention and care are necessary for very young children. Most child-care centers won't accept infants unless they cater exclusively to babies.

Once your child has developed communication skills and socializing has become more important, center-based child care will look more attractive, especially when it offers educational, cultural, or religious activities. There are a variety of child-care options available for working parents, both in and outside the home.

In-Home Child Care: Pros and Cons

For some people, it's appealing to have someone come to or live in your home to care for your child. Your baby's routine is not disturbed; you just go to work without any problems of delivering your baby to a center. This well may be the solution for you. As with everything else though, there are advantages and disadvantages to this kind of child care:

Advantages:
- Some in-home caregivers will help with housework and meals.
- You set your own rules.
- You can call home anytime without worrying about disturbing some activity at a center.
- You have fewer worries about your baby catching any contagious diseases.
- You're free for business travel if the caregiver is willing to stay overnight.
- Your baby gets individual care and can establish a close bond with a caregiver.
- Your baby remains in a familiar setting.

Disadvantages:
- The cost is high.
- You must provide a bedroom for a live-in caregiver.
- You have responsibility for benefits, withholding, and other paperwork (see "Caring for Your Caregiver," page 257).
- You lose your privacy with a live-in caregiver.
- You need a backup when your caregiver is sick.

• There are no training programs, except for some nanny services.
• Some working mothers become jealous of their caregiver's time with their baby.

In spite of the benefits of individualized child care in your home, there is no guarantee of your baby's safety. In-home caregivers are not supervised as in a center. In some communities, a caregiver is isolated from your neighbors and friends. In other words, you have to be very sure that the person you hire is experienced and trustworthy.

Outside-the-Home Child Care: Pros and Cons

Child care in your home is possible only if your income and/or accommodations are large enough. For most new working parents, therefore, the alternative is group care outside their home. Both public agencies and private organizations provide child care. Some must conform to local or state regulations mandating a license. In general, the younger a baby is, the fewer places are available for group care.

The Three Categories of Group Care

The Office of Child Development of the U.S. Department of Health and Human Services defines three basic types of group care:

• *Comprehensive child development programs*—These programs meet all the needs of the growing children and their families: education, nutrition and health, family counseling, and instruction in child development.

- *Custodial care*—At the other extreme, these centers provide little more than baby-sitting services.

- *Developmental care*—Children have many opportunities for social and educational development in these programs. Trained people work with good books and educational toys. The programs offer nutritionally sound meals and medical care when necessary.

FYI: Government Help for Child Care

In 1990, Congress—recognizing what working parents have already known for years, that productivity suffers, absenteeism grows, and workers are forced to quit jobs when they lack adequate child care—passed the first comprehensive child-care legislation in two decades, the Child Care and Development Block Grant.

This grant is currently the major source of federal government subsidy for child care for low-income working parents. While the funding is still not enough to meet the needs of all America's lower-income families, it might generate some improvement in the quality of the nation's child care, including at least a minimal upgrading of some state health and safety protection for lower-income families. Contact your state or county human services agency for more information regarding this grant.

Grading Group Care for Your Child

As with any other choices in life, group child care for your baby while you work has its drawbacks and its benefits. Each working couple has to decide what factors are going to weigh most heavily in their decision.

Advantages:
- Costs are lower than individual care. (Some centers are subsidized for low-income families.)
- It's a social experience for your child and a chance for you to meet other parents in the same position.
- You don't have to worry about a caregiver being ill or quitting.
- It has stimulating materials for your child that you might not have at home.
- Many centers are government regulated, ensuring minimum standards of safety, sanitation, and supervision.
- Teachers are usually well trained in early child development.

Disadvantages:
- You have less control over the environment.
- You're responsible for transporting your child to and from the center.
- Some centers close during school holidays.
- Large group size may be hard on your young child.
- The routine may be more rigid than at home.
- Your child may be confused by the lack of continuity in teachers.
- Some centers are resistant to storing and preparing breast milk.
- Understaffing, or poor staffing, may be a problem.
- The center may not accept babies less than one year.
- Your child may be exposed to contagious diseases.

- Many centers will not take a sick child.
- Coordinating your work hours with the center's hours may be difficult. You may have to arrange for care before and after your child attends the center.

FYI: Who is Caring for Our Children?

The true figures for child care would have to include all unlicensed caregivers as well as those who are licensed. It is estimated that two out of three caregivers are unlicensed. The following statistics that have been gathered for licensed workers show only how great the need is for adequate child-care services:

- *Of all children under three years of age, 50 percent are cared for in other people's homes.*
- *Forty-seven percent of children three to six years old are cared for in other people's homes. Child-care facilities care for another 15 percent, and 38 percent go to nursery school for part of the day, and then spend the balance of the day at home with their mother, or a baby-sitter, or with their mother in the work place.*
- *Most child-care workers are paid less than poverty-level wages (often with no benefits) so it's no wonder turnover is as high as 75 percent.*
- *Obviously, the need for licensed child-care facilities is not being met. For the thirty million American children with working parents, only 905,000 licensed child-care spaces are available, a ratio of thirty to one.*

The Facts about Supplemental Care

While research on the effect of supplemental care on infants is still in the early stages because the great call for child care is a rather recent phenomenon, the Panel on Work, Family and Community found that there is no compelling evidence to suggest that working parents automatically bring negative consequences to their children. To the contrary, studies show that babies in day care show a remarkable capacity for "initiative learning." Only when children were placed in low-quality care with a high ratio of babies to caregivers, with untrained personnel, and with a high turnover of personnel did children suffer any maladjustments.

Recent research shows that the amount of time children spend in quality infant day-care programs is positively related to how well the children fare both socially and emotionally in elementary school. In several studies, the children who spent the most time in quality day care had more friends, spent more time in extracurricular activities, and demonstrated more assertiveness and leadership ability than other elementary school children. Experts found that these children were more likely to end up in gifted programs in school, to excel in math classes, and to be more socially skilled.

Chapter 13

Choosing Child Care That Meets Your Needs

The first three years of a baby's life have a profound effect on his or her physical and emotional development. Because many working parents are away from their babies for up to forty-five hours a week, a caregiver's responses to a child are crucial in the building of a child's self-esteem. While no one else can advise you on the best child care for your particular situation, if you go about making a choice in a careful, organized way, you're more likely to make the right one.

Starting the Selection Process

The best approach to finding good child care is to start early, before your baby is born. Look around to see what's available and ask other working parents. If you find a good situation, make an advance deposit on tuition or pay a portion of the salary. In other words, don't let the good one get away.

QUESTIONS TO ASK YOURSELF AS YOU ASSESS YOUR NEEDS

You may find that your options narrow down quickly on the basis of availability and cost. These questions will help you think about your basic needs:

1. When do I want child care to begin?

2. How old will my child be?

3. What will the caregiver's hours be?
   Consider how long you'll be gone from home, whether your hours will vary, whether you'll need overnight help, and what days of the week you must cover.

4. How much can I afford?

5. What options are available?

6. How long do I want this arrangement to last?

7. Do I want child care close to my job? Close to my partner's job?

8. Will I need someone year round or only part of the year?

9. Where would I accommodate live-in help? How much would it cost to remodel?

Get Recommendations

You may have your own sources of information, but in case you're at a loss for ideas, here are some places to turn to for referrals:

- State day-care licensing board, department of health or welfare

- Your personnel officer

- Children's advocacy group

- Day-care referral service (see "Use an Agency," below) or support group for children with special needs

- YMCA or American Red Cross for lists of people who have passed their baby-sitting courses

- High school, college, or nursing school

- Senior citizen group

- Pediatrician

- Temples or churches

- Supermarket, library, or laundromat bulletin boards

• Chamber of commerce

• Yellow Pages under child-care referral, social services, or community coordinated child care

Use Classified Ads

Look for ads seeking child-care jobs or place an ad yourself. Evaluate prospective employees over the phone (see "Save Time with Phone Interviews," page 228) and limit your personal interviews to only the most qualified. A help wanted ad might read like this:

> Child-care giver wanted. Mature, loving, experienced caregiver needed to care for infant in home, Monday–Friday, 7:30 a.m.–5:30 p.m. (State responsibilities and salary). Reliable transportation and references a must. Call 555-2222 evenings.

Use an Agency

To avoid time-consuming phone calls, use a child-care agency. Some are commercial agencies and others are sponsored by organizations. There are no national standards for child-care agencies; therefore, do your own research to evaluate the agencies before using them. Check with your state Department of Consumer Affairs or the Better Business Bureau to find out if any complaints have been filed against them. When you've located one with a good reputation, interview the manager by phone. Following are questions you will want to ask:

1. How many years have you been in the child-care business?

2. Are you a member of any specific organizations or associations?

3. Are you bonded or licensed (a requirement in some but not all states)?

4. What are your screening procedures?

5. Are the interviews and reference checks done over the phone or in person?

6. How many references do you require?

7. Will you give me access to all the information you have?

8. What is your fee and how and when is it payable? (Typically, agencies charge a placement fee of one month's salary.)

9. What happens if I hire someone and it doesn't work out? Do I get all money back, just a portion, or will you find another caregiver for me? (Many agencies offer a refund—less a percentage—or a free replacement within a limited period, usually thirty to sixty days.)

10. Do you provide a written work agreement?

You can appraise an agency further by noting how carefully they screen you. The more questions they ask about your needs, the closer they can come to supplying a suitable candidate. Describe your needs in detail. A good agency will follow through after a candidate's interview by calling you.

Now that child care is such an issue, a new kind of agency has been sprouting up around the country. These agencies are called information and referral services (I & R) or resource and referral agencies (R & R). These operations provide working parents with reliable information about good child-care people and places in the community. They also counsel parents to help the parents decide what kind of child care would fit their family circumstances.

Save Time with Phone Interviews
Whether you choose an in-home caregiver or an outside child-care facility, you can weed out unsuitable applicants in a minimum amount of time on the phone during your work breaks.

Interviewing the Individual In-Home Caregiver by Telephone
Cover these points in your telephone interview with an in-home caregiver:

- Your child's description

- Your needs

- The applicant's experience and with children of what age

• The applicant's housekeeping experience

• The length of former jobs and reason for leaving

• References (and their phone numbers) from at least three former employers

Take into consideration these three points as you accept or reject initial applicants:

1. *Language skills*—Does the applicant have a sufficient command of English for you to be able to communicate clearly? Would you be able to supervise your child's care by phone?

2. *Telephone skills*—Does the applicant have telephone skills? Don't be too quick to judge an applicant by her telephone personality, though. Some people sound remote or slow-witted on the phone because they lack confidence.

3. *Answering machine*—If you're tempted to use the answering machine to take calls, you might lose a good caregiver because the machine is intimidating. When a face-to-face interview isn't possible, such as with an au pair in another country, have several telephone conversations until you feel at ease.

Important Tips for Checking References

As a working woman, you know that employment references are important. They are just as critical, if not more so, when you're choosing someone to be in your home caring for your baby. Be sure to check and recheck the references you're given. Here are a few basic pointers:

1. Speak with former employers directly; never accept a letter as the sole reference.
2. Reject anyone you suspect of using a friend or a relative as a work reference.
3. Be careful if the person you're referred to seems reluctant to answer your questions.
4. Verify information about previous job responsibilities, hours, and salary. Also confirm the reason for leaving.
5. Ask about the applicant's relations with the children, what they liked and disliked about the applicant, and how the applicant worked out problems.
6. Ask the former employer to rate the applicant in terms of time management and whether she was a good role model.
7. Ask a last question, whether the former employer would hire the applicant again.
8. Leave your phone number in case she or he thinks of something else.

Interviewing Child-Care Facilities by Telephone

Before you visit a center, save yourself time by phoning in advance and asking about these particulars:

- *Location*—It doesn't matter how good the center is; if it's too far from work or home, forget it. Otherwise, your daily drive to and from work will be too time consuming.

- *Fees*—If you are in a financial pinch, don't be shy about asking to defer payment for a month or two, or requesting a guarantee that fees won't increase over the next year. You may be able to work out a more flexible, cost-saving schedule as well.

- *Schedule*—Are the hours convenient for your work schedule? Does the facility close for summer vacations, extreme weather, or holidays?

- *Operating policies*—How is it staffed? Does it encourage parent involvement? What ages are the children?

- *Openings*—Many centers have waiting lists. If you like what you hear and what you see later when you visit, sign up at once or add your name to a waiting list. Keep looking around if you're not sure your name will come up by the time you want to return to work. Visit centers that sound good even if they don't anticipate any openings. A good program can teach you what to look for in other centers.

Of course, you won't rely on a phone call for making your final judgment. Arrange for personal interviews only with the centers that you're enthusiastic about.

Interviewing an In-Home Caregiver

Evaluating an individual applicant for the demanding job of caring for your child depends less on policies and programs—as with a day-care center—than on the personality and experience of the prospective caregiver.

Outside of family members, you should first interview a caregiver in your home. Once you have several potential candidates, you and your spouse should conduct an interview. Keep the following points in mind when you're interviewing:

- *Ask for proof*—Ask a non-citizen to bring a passport and proof of legal status. If any driving is involved, ask to see a valid driver's license.

- *Ask your partner to attend interviews or schedule them at a time when he's home*—Both of you will have to work with this employee.

- *Have your baby with you*—Give each applicant a chance to interact with your baby. But also have a baby-sitter on hand so that you have a chance to talk without interruption. Try to avoid interviewing at your baby's fussy time.

- *Ask questions*—Ask each applicant the same questions so that you can make fair comparisons. Find out about education, child-care training and experience (see "Caregiver Questionnaire" on the following pages).

- *Examine values and experience*—Ask open-ended questions, such as what she would do if...? That way you'll be able to judge the person's experience and values. Ask about background, childhood experiences, and schooling. People tend to interact with children in the same way they were raised.

- *Be noncommittal*—Encourage the applicant to do most of the talking. If you reveal your attitudes, you're more likely to hear what the applicant thinks you want to hear.

CAREGIVER QUESTIONNAIRE

Name _____ Phone _____

Address _____

_____

Recommended by _____

Interview Date _____ Starting Date _____

1st Referral _____ Phone _____

Comments _____

2nd Referral _____ Phone _____

Comments _____

3rd Referral _____ Phone _____

Comments _____

Background

What is your job history? _____

Why did you leave your last job? _____

Is it included in your references? _____

What were the ages of the children you cared for? _____

Do you have any physical limitations that would affect your work? _____

_____

Have you been vaccinated against the common childhood diseases? _____

_____

How many sick days did you have to take off from work over the past year? __

For personal reasons?_____

Do you know CPR? _____

First Aid? _____

Do you belong to any child-care organization, group, or network? _____

_____

Philosophies

What do you find to be the most difficult thing about caring for babies?_____

_____

What are your feelings about:

Feeding: _____

Disciplining: _____

Crying: _____

Pacifiers/security objects: _____

Other: _____

Why do you enjoy being with babies? _____

What kinds of activities do you enjoy most? _____

_____

Responsibilities

Would you be living in or out? _____

(If the applicant is going to be living in, find out why she wants this situation. If she is to live out, discuss any problems that might cause delays in the morning.)

Do you have a valid driver's license? _____

Can you drive a standard shift as well as an automatic?_____

(If she'll be chauffeuring your child around town, obtain a copy of her driving record from the state Department of Motor Vehicles.)

Do you enjoy cooking? Meal planning? _____

Grocery shopping? _____

Will you do housework? _____

Anything you won't do?_____

Wages/Benefits

What type of weekly/monthly wage do you want?_____

How many paid sick and vacations days do you expect? _____

What holidays do you want to have off? _____

Do you have health insurance or would you expect us to provide it?_____

Expectations

How long a commitment could you make to our family?_____

What are your long-term goals? _____

_____

Could you stay late occasionally if an emergency comes up and I can't get home on time? _____

Would you expect payment in return, time off, or both?_____

Other expectations: _____

_____

When you interview a caregiver, watch how she reacts to your child and how your child reacts to her. (This is one of your best means of judging an applicant, so pay careful attention.) Then at the end of the interview, ask yourself these questions:

- Does she seem comfortable?
- Does she seem competent and experienced?
- How does she respond to my child?
- My child to her?
- Does she seem gentle?
- Does she communicate well?
- Will she be able to remember and follow directions, including written instructions? (If possible, subtly find out how well the applicant reads and writes.)
- Does she seem dependable?
- Did she come on time?
- If not, did she phone promptly to say she'd be late?
- Did she have trouble with directions?
- Did she sound intelligent, with thoughts of her own, or did she spout theories about the proper way to bring up children?
- Could you imagine her in your home with your child?
- Is she too rigid, too clean? (You don't want someone who is fanatical or always compulsive with your child.)
- Does she answer questions monosyllabically, evasively, or without consistent eye contact?
- How does she look?

- Is she neat and clean?
- Does she seem confused, unclear, or simply hard to understand?
- Does she seem troubled by any personal problems?

Notes:_____

_____

_____

_____

_____

What to Do after the Interview

When someone isn't suitable, politely say thank you and explain that you think this is not the right arrangement for you. Note your impressions and keep a file of your questionnaires. Always conduct second interviews with likely candidates. Vital information may emerge on a second interview when everyone is a little more relaxed. Judge applicants on their experience and the extent to which they meet your requirements. Trust your instincts and don't compromise.

Narrowing Your Choices

Choose the best of the candidates and ask each one to provide a letter of clearance from the State Bureau of Investigation and the child abuse agency that keeps records of reported child abuse. Also, ask for the applicant's agreement to take a physical exam at your expense.

When you're down to the final choices, ask each one to work for a day or so while you're still home. That should help you with the final choice.

Writing a Contract

As a working woman, you've already developed the habit of putting things in writing. It will serve you well in this instance, too. Be sure to include the following points in your contract:

- *Duties*—List all responsibilities including specific tasks and how often you want them done.

- *Salary*—Include weekly salary, or hourly wage, raises, vacation time, holidays, overtime wages, and other benefits, as well as how much notice is required to terminate the contract.

- *Time schedules*—Note rest periods, mealtimes, and time off for personal activities when your caregiver is living in.

- *Other policies*—Spell out policies regarding illness, trips outside the house, transportation, and telephone privileges.

- *Live-in accommodations*—Describe the room and bathroom facility provided, telephone provision, and use of the family car.

- *Ask her to sign a Child-Care Planner*—Make sure there is no misunderstanding as to how she is to care for your child. Use the planner on the following pages as your guide.

CHILD-CARE PLANNER

Child's Name: _____

Feeding

    What to Feed:_____

    When to Feed: _____

    Nutrition Guidelines: _____

    Safety: _____

Sleep

    Schedule: _____

    Pre-sleep Routine: _____

    Rules: _____

Diapering

    Schedule: _____

    Routine: _____

Potty Training

    Schedule: _____

    Discipline: _____

    Methods: _____

Play

    Favorite Activities: _____

    Favorite Projects: _____

    Favorite Places to Go: _____

    Favorite Toys: _____

    Favorite Books: _____

Television and Video

Television: _____

Programs/Videos: _____

Okay to Watch:_____

_____ Times a Day

Visitors

Personal Visitors for Caregiver: _____

Special Needs and Medications: _____

(See "What to Do If Your Child is Sick or Injured," page 267)

Interviewing a Child-Care Center or Family Home

Family day care is used more frequently by parents of very young children. In fact, one-third of employed mothers with children under age five rely on care arrangements in which the caregiver takes care of several children in her own home. The actual definition of family day care varies, though it typically refers to a private home in which the resident provides care for four to six young children.

In order to recognize a high-quality child-care center or family home, you should first become acquainted with the standards for judging policies, procedures, and programs. Keep the following information in mind when selecting a child-care site.

Licensing and Accreditation

State monitoring agencies, which oversee licensing and/or accreditation standards, vary greatly in their effectiveness. Their purpose is to ensure that a child-care facility meets the state's minimum requirements for health and safety standards at the time of the inspection. The trouble is that inspectors make few repeat inspections, so you can't depend on the facility's license unquestioningly.

Nine out of ten family day-care homes are unlicensed and unknown to the state. Some of them don't apply for a license because they don't want bureaucrats snooping around. Others want to avoid the expense of remodeling to meet the state code. Still others want to avoid paying taxes on their income.

Unfortunately, these caregivers isolate themselves from other people in the business and from government resources that could help them offer better care. To remedy this situation, many communities have turned to voluntary registration of family child-care providers and their agreement to meet minimum standards. The parents who send their children to these homes, nevertheless, must monitor to see that the following standards are met at all times.

Group Size and Child-Teacher Ratio

These factors are usually also regulated by the state. Here, too, standards vary by the state, but the following guidelines should help:

- *Infant to two years*—Every four children should have an adult supervisor; maximum group size is six to eight.

- *Two to three years*—Every six toddlers should have an adult supervisor; maximum group size is ten to twelve.

- *Three to four years*—One adult can supervise twelve preschoolers; the maximum size for the group is sixteen.

In a family day-care home, five children is the maximum for one adult, with no more than two children under two years of age.

Staff Criteria

The staff members of an established child-care center, at a minimum, should have some training in child care and an interest in improving their skills through reading, course work, and membership in a professional organization. The director should have a degree in early childhood development or a child development associate's certificate. Look for these features too:

- *Turnover*—The turnover rate should be less than 25 percent. If staff members stay a year or more, that's a good sign. Ask staff people how long they've been working in child care, and if they intend to continue.

- *Criminal background*—Especially in a family day-care home, you want to know whether anyone has a criminal record. Consult criminal-record databases, and ask if background checks have been run on all employees. You can conduct your own background check by obtaining records from the Department of Motor Vehicles.

- *Salary*—Salaries are among the best indicators of quality. Ask about salaries and medical benefits. Employees with medical benefits are more likely to obtain preventive care and less likely to come to work sick.

- *Personality*—Caregivers should be affectionate, patient, and enthusiastic. They should interact with the children frequently and participate in play at the children's level. Look for a cooperative spirit.

- *Good health*—Caregivers should be in good mental and physical health. The center should administer psychological screening before they're hired and require physical exams at least every two years.

Program/Curriculum Standards

All programs in a child-care center should be developmentally appropriate for the age of the children. Many centers post a daily schedule or publish a copy in the parents' handbook. Even when a schedule is followed, no child should be forced to participate in any activity. Inquire whether any special measures are taken to make a new child feel comfortable (see "Seven Ways to Help Your Child Adjust to a Child-Care Site," page 256). Also, check on these components:

- *Record-keeping*—Records are kept for each child. Also, parents are kept informed of their child's progress on a regular schedule. If your child misbehaves, the staff should discuss it with you.

- *Goal-setting*—Goals are set for development at all levels: physical, social, language, and intellectual.

- *Balanced activity*—A balance is kept between indoor and outdoor play and between active games and quiet times. A variety of stimulating, age-appropriate toys and games are provided, as well as safe, washable toys for babies. Look for many books and ask about reading out loud times.

- *Nurturing*—Are babies held and talked to often?

- *Learning assessments*—Each child is screened for early identification of learning difficulties.

The people who run a child-care center or home should always be open to your comments and suggestions. If you sense a lack of interest in what you have to say, question their desire to improve their services.

FYI: Help for Judging the Standards for Child Care

Health and safety standards differ so widely from state to state that most professional health organizations have joined to create the first national, comprehensive standards for child-care centers. The American Academy of Pediatrics and the American Public Health Association, in their four-hundred-page book, address the needs of children up to age twelve on such topics as staffing, age-appropriate activities, and safety precautions, in addition to food service and health policies. Ask your child-care facility, library, or pediatrician's office to order a copy.

Questions about Costs

The cost of child care varies widely, of course, depending on location, local standards, and types of services offered. You can expect to pay from 25 to 50 percent more for infant care. Use this rule of thumb to determine what you can afford: Child care should cost no more than 12 percent of your income. Ask these questions to be sure you get the whole picture:

1. How do I pay the fees: in advance, weekly, or monthly?
2. Do you have scholarships and financial-aid programs?
3. Will you charge extra if I bring my child early or if I get there late?
4. Do you charge when we're on vacation?
5. Are there special rates for two or more children in a family?

6. Do you charge when a child is home ill?

7. Do you provide receipts for a tax credit?

Feeding Concerns

Make sure these six procedures and philosophies are followed:

1. Babies are fed in caregivers' arms and never with a propped-up bottle.

2. Caregivers are familiar with the handling of breast milk. They need to take the time to use a cup, dropper, or spoon if your baby refuses a bottle.

3. Breast milk is stored safely.

4. Private space is provided for breast-feeding.

5. Older children are fed healthy food, and special food needs are accommodated.

6. Finger feeding is encouraged.

Health Policies

Child-care facilities must be meticulous about health concerns. Policies should be in place regarding the treatment of mildly ill children and the limits on attendance for sick children. They must require immunization records too. In addition, a child-care center or home should follow these methods:

- *Medications*—Medical information about each child is clearly posted where all staff members can see it. Medications are kept in original containers, properly labeled.

- *Emergencies*—An emergency plan is drawn up that designates someone for hospital transport in case of serious injury or illness. That person should have a child's car seat.

- *Medical care*—A nearby doctor is designated to be on call. Emergency numbers are posted near all telephones. Someone on the staff must be trained in CPR and first aid.

- *Sanitation*—Caregivers are trained to wash hands after every diapering and before every feeding. Soiled diapers are kept in sealed, plastic-lined containers. Diapering areas, toilets, and feeding areas are cleaned and sanitized every day. Children's hands are washed before meals.

- *Beds*—Children sleep in separate beds; linens are changed frequently.

- *Rest*—Times for rest are provided every day with an adult supervising.

Safety Procedures

Make sure the following steps have been taken at every child-care site to protect the children from harm:

- The facility is well-lighted and provides adequate heat. Hazardous items, dangerous obstacles, poisons, and small objects that can be swallowed have been removed.

- At least thirty-five square feet of crawling space is provided for each infant and seventy-five square feet of outdoor play space is provided for each child.

- The play space is protected from animal contamination, which includes covering the sandbox when not in use. (If any pets are in the home, will your child have contact with them?)

- Stairways are blocked, fences are secured, and play areas are enclosed.

- Broken furniture, toys, or other equipment have been repaired.

- Soft-landing surfaces under swings and other playthings are provided.

- Bolt and other hardware are securely fastened and covered with smooth rounded edges.

- Art materials are nontoxic.

- An emergency evacuation plan has been established and it is practiced monthly. Emergency exits are clearly marked.

- Parking lot and loading zones are clean and safe.

- Smoke detectors and fire extinguishers are provided in every room.

• Swimming pools, ponds, and decorative fountains are covered or fenced off.

• A stranger is never allowed to collect a child unless there is written permission from a parent.

FYI: Child Care and Safety

A study by the Centers for Disease Control, a major federal research facility in Atlanta, shows that young children are injured less frequently in child care than they are in their homes. Apparently, the structured, controlled, child-proof environment of a child-care center works better to prevent injuries. The researchers also found that child-care children were less likely to be poisoned.

The Question of Discipline

No spanking or other corporal punishment should ever be used by a caregiver. Shouting, shaming, or withholding of food should never be employed to discipline children. Reasonable discipline can be maintained at a child-care center or home by supervising carefully, setting clear limits, using a "time out" corner, and explaining in age-appropriate ways that certain behavior is not permitted.

Respond immediately if you ever suspect that something disturbing is happening at child care. Visit the center or home as soon as you can take time off from work to find out what's going on. If you can't take the time from work to check out your child-care situation, ask a friend or family member to help you out (see "Protecting Your Child from Abuse," page 263).

What to Look for When You Visit a Child-Care Facility

Plan to visit each facility for at least a half an hour. You can take your lunch hour for these inspections. If you encounter any objections to your desire to look around for a while, cross this place off your list. Your evaluation should include these areas:

- *Interview*—Arrange for a meeting with the person in charge. Discuss the center's child-raising philosophy and compare it with your own.

- *Written information*—Ask to see a sample listing of daily activities and weekly menus, as well as a copy of operating policies.

- *Parent references*—Ask for phone numbers of other parents and follow up with calls.

- *Interactions*—Note the interaction among parents, children, and care-givers at drop-off and pick-up times. The staff member should deal with children's separation anxiety in a professional manner (see "Overcoming Back-to-Work Anxieties," page 294).

- *Atmosphere*—Do the children look happy? If the staff works to create a loving, family atmosphere, the children will respond to it.

- *Equipment*—Note the amount and kind of stimulation that's provided for the children.

CHILD-CARE CENTER WORKSHEET

Make a photocopy of this form and bring it along to each center or family day-care home you visit. Be sure to let them know that you're using the worksheet to help you recall what you've seen and asked. Your notes will help you to remember each place accurately and guard against confusing one place with another. Be suspicious if your questions aren't freely answered.

Name of center/home _____

Name of director/owner _____

Address _____

_____Phone _____

Referred by _____Phone _____

1st Recommendation _____Phone _____

Comments _____

_____

2nd Recommendation_____Phone _____

Comments _____

_____

Operating policies

Hours of operation _____Visiting times _____

Licensed/Registered/Other No._____

Costs _____

Staff/caregiver

Ratio of children to caregivers _____ Staff turnover rate _____

Caregiver's background _____

_____

Program

Goals _____

Nutrition _____

Feeding _____

Safety_____

Health _____

Notes: _____

_____

_____

_____

_____

FYI: Finding Accredited Centers

Two national organizations are now accrediting day-care centers. The National Association of Child-Care Resource and Referral Agencies will send you a list of all the referral agencies and support groups in your state and local area. Also, the National Association for the Education of Young Children will send you a list of accredited day-care centers.

Make a Second Visit

When you've narrowed the field to two or three good choices, return for a second visit before you make your final decision. After your child is attending for a month or so, evaluate how well she or he has adjusted. You might want to consider another care site if the adjustment is poor.

Easing the Back-to-Work Transition

When you return to work, allow some time for a transition period. The optimal transition time is two weeks: One for you to teach your baby's caregiver your methods and allow her to become comfortable in your home, and one for the caregiver to take over while you're still there to answer questions. Of course, some working women simply can't take that kind of time. If that's your situation, at least try to spend the first couple of days at home. You want to make sure that the caregiver is comfortable with your infant.

Always make sure your baby sees you and the caregiver together. Never leave without saying good-bye to your child and explaining that you're going (see "Helping Your Baby and Yourself with Separation Anxiety," page 303). Routines are very important to babies. Don't leave before you've explained all of them to the caregiver.

Basic Rules for Safety in Your Home
Unfortunately, these days you have to worry about the safety of those you leave behind when you go off to work. Teach your caregiver to take certain basic precautions, such as:

- Lock all the doors after you leave.

- Never allow strangers or visitors in the house unless they've been approved by you first.

- Call the police if prowlers are suspected.

- Tell any callers that you're unavailable and ask to take a message. Never say that you're not home.

- Keep phone calls to a minimum.

- Never leave children unattended.

- Don't smoke.

• Understand the escape plan in case of a fire.

Seven Ways to Help Your Child Adjust to a Child-Care Site

1. *Absent yourself*—For a least a month in advance, accustom your child to your absence and the presence of a caregiver by staying away for increasingly longer periods.

2. *Visit the center or home*—Shortly before child care is to begin, take your child for an hour's visit to meet the other children and the teachers. Show your child the layout of the care site; play a little with the toys and equipment.

3. *Talk about the details*—Each day talk about going to the care site. Tell a child who is old enough to understand about the details of a day at the center. Start with dressing in the morning and go through the activities of the day one by one. End up by describing how you will be there at the end of the day.

4. *Dress your child appropriately*—Send your child in clothes that can get dirty and are easily cleaned. Your infant will need two to three changes of clothes daily. Be sure to label all items with your child's name.

5. *Write a schedule*—Give the care site a written schedule of your baby's routine.

6. *Supply everything needed*—Bring everything that your baby needs or might need to the center or home. It's much easier than having to leave work to get some forgotten, yet vital, item. Mark formula or medicine bottles, for instance, with your baby's name.

7. *Stay for awhile*—If you can possibly spare the time from work, stay with your child at the care site for a few minutes in the morning. Once your child is engrossed in play, it'll be easier to leave.

Caring for Your Caregiver

A good relationship with a caregiver requires cooperation and open communication. With a live-in caregiver, employer and employee must learn to share a closeness while respecting each other's privacy. With a child-care center or home, you must keep up your share of the responsibility and aid in the smooth functioning of the program. Show your caregiver that you appreciate every effort by keeping these things in mind:

• *Be prompt*—Always be on time or call if you are delayed. Pay all your caregiver wages and fees as soon as they're due.

• *Be fair*—Don't ask for domestic tasks that weren't part of the agreement. Assure your live-in caregiver that she has all promised time off and hire a baby-sitter if necessary. Offer to pay overtime when you're late.

- *Be considerate*—Provide a comfortable, attractive room of her own. Giving her a phone (she pays the bill) and a TV of her own will help to avoid any conflicts and maintain privacy for everyone. Stock the pantry with the caregiver's favorite foods. Help to relieve her isolation by arranging introductions to other caregivers in the neighborhood. Call her by her preferred name.

- *Be generous*—Offer something extra now and then: An afternoon off, an evening class, a dinner, or a memento when you've been on a business trip. If you pay somewhat more than the going rate, your caregiver will probably be willing to give you something extra in return. Be liberal with your praise and understanding and don't forget to say thank you.

- *Be respectful*—Always treat your employees with respect, especially a live-in caregiver who functions almost as a member of your family. Show confidence in her judgment and respect your differences. Her way may not be your way, but don't interfere unless an important issue is involved. Think of your caregiver as your partner; don't undermine her authority with your child. Schedule conferences at least twice a year where you take the time to talk about your child's development and resolve any differences.

- *Be clear*—Talk about your attitudes towards child rearing with your caregiver and what kind of care you expect. Plan your child's day together. Ask her to keep a log of the day's activities. Your child's needs will change—discuss together how they will be addressed. Phone home often, especially in the early stages of the relationship. Regular chats allow you to keep track of what's happening and give your caregiver opportunity to air her concerns.

• *Communicate*—Ask questions about your child's day and then listen to the answers; you might hear something surprising. Be honest and direct, never accusatory. Always offer helpful critiques of her performance in private.

• *Keep your caregiver informed of family news that might affect your child's behavior*—Let her know in advance of planned vacations or business trips, or of the guests you're expecting. Ask questions about her family, and once you feel at ease, her opinions on child rearing.

• *Be flexible*—As your baby's needs change as time passes, so will you caregiver's duties. Stay flexible and open to new ways of doing things.

• *Be sensitive*—Your caregiver may have hidden issues you should understand: Perhaps a feeling, still common in our society, that mothers shouldn't work outside the home, or a feeling of a lower value because she must stay in the house while you leave every day. If you suspect a hidden issue, try to get to the bottom of it before there's trouble.

Wages, Hours, and Benefits

People tend to economize on child care, but that's a false economy. You should spend as much as you can to hire the best possible care for your child. A caregiver will usually set a rate for her services based on several factors: training, experience, her duties, whether she's affiliated with an agency, and of course, the current wage level in your area.

Determine what that is by asking around at work and among your friends. A caregiver who works in your home is at least entitled to the federal minimum wage. In some states, the minimum wage level is even higher than the federal. Ask your State Department of Labor.

The Urban League regards forty-four hours as the typical work week for a live-in worker and forty hours at eight hours a day for a live-out worker. Any time over that should be paid for at time and a half, and any time over fifty-two hours at double time. Another option is to pay for overtime work with compensatory time off, although that gets to be hard to arrange in a two-worker family.

Do you remember how good you felt when you received your last raise? You felt valued and felt your efforts were validated. You may even have promised yourself to make an extra effort on the job in the future. Keep in mind that your caregiver needs the same reinforcement. Your employment agreement with her should include an annual raise in pay.

Taxes and Withholding

Every employer, according to law, must plan on withholding and paying income taxes, social security payments, unemployment insurance, and in some states, worker's compensation payments for employees who earn more than fifty dollars in a three-month period. Check with an accountant regarding your state's requirements.

FYI—Paying Your Caregiver "Off the Books"

It's been common practice to pay caregivers "under the table." This gives the caregiver more take-home pay and saves the employer many hours of tax-withholding and other paper work. But the Internal Revenue Service calls this tax evasion, and they will pursue any suspects and levy penalties if they can prove the law was broken. Before you take this route, consider that at some time in the future, your employee might decide to file for Social Security. If she can prove prior earnings as your caregiver, you could be liable for many years of interest and penalties, in addition to the unpaid taxes.

Medical Insurance

If your caregiver doesn't have access to health care through a spouse's insurance or a group insurance plan, help her to join an organization that includes health insurance for their members. Investigate membership in the National Association for the Education of Young Children, an organization of early-childhood education professionals, parents, and others concerned with young children. The NAEYC offers such a plan.

Sick Leave

While sick leave is discretionary, one paid sick day a year is fair for the number of days a week a part-time caregiver works after a one-year period.

As an example, if your caregiver works three days a week, she should be given three paid sick days. A full-time employee should receive a minimum of six paid sick days annually.

Auto Insurance

You may have to add your caregiver's name to your auto insurance policy. Before you do, check her driving record and ask your insurance broker about your state's requirements.

Vacations and Holidays

Give your full-time caregiver two weeks' paid vacation after one year on the job. Part-time employees get one day's paid vacation for each working day a week. Ideally, your caregiver should take vacation time when you and your family are on vacation. If this arrangement does not fit in with her plans, you'll have to hire a substitute caregiver while she's on vacation. Some families take their caregiver with them on vacation to watch the children. Keep in mind, however, this is a working period for the caregiver. You still have to arrange for vacation time at some other date.

Eight paid legal holidays a year is the standard for full-time, live-in caregivers, six days for live-out, full-time workers. Part-time employees should receive one paid legal holiday a year for each full day's work in a week. Your own holidays will guide you in negotiating which ones your caregiver takes.

Changing Your Caregiver

There are usually two reasons for changing your child-care arrangements. Either it's time for a change in type of care, say, from individual to group, or your caregiver is unsatisfactory. In the first instance, give your caregiver plenty of notice, from two weeks to a month, and don't forget severance pay. Depending on how long she's been with you, one or two weeks' pay and accumulated vacation pay is sufficient. You're under no legal obligation to furnish a letter of reference. Legal experts say the letter should contain only dates of employment, anyway.

When the parting is less than amicable, furnish the same severance pay and ask the caregiver to leave immediately. You don't want a resentful person caring for your child. Now is the time for your emergency back-up system to fall into place or for you to get a temporary worker from a household-help agency. It's expensive, but on a short term basis it may be the best solution.

Changing your caregiver won't be easy under any conditions. Working parents, not to mention their children, become very dependent on their caregivers. If your break with the caregiver is sudden, you'll have to start all over from the beginning to find someone else whom you trust and whom your baby likes.

Protecting Your Child from Abuse

A young child has no defenses against abusive treatment of any nature. You have an obligation, when your child is being cared for by another, to be alert for warning signs of trouble, such as the following:

- *Anxiety*—If your child becomes anxious, fearful, or withdrawn and passive, it may indicate a response to a frightening experience.

- *Constipation*—Harsh toilet training may cause a child to withhold bowel movements until regularity is upset.

- *Diaper rash*—A severe diaper rash might indicate that diapers are not being changed often enough.

- *Bruising*—Ask how the bruise was caused. If your child isn't talking yet, ask the caregiver for an explanation.

- *Boredom*—An infant who's propped up in an infant seat most of the day is not getting enough stimulation. Look for a rubbed spot on the back of his neck, or crankiness, or a lack of response to smiles.

- *Exhaustion*—Some caregivers provide too much stimulation with noise and games going all day long with little rest. Does your baby have trouble settling down into your family's evening routine? Perhaps over-stimulation is the case.

How to Solve the Problem

It's not easy to judge whether a young child is telling an accurate story or what a bruise on an infant means, but you can't afford to ignore these warning signs. You need to take the following steps:

- *Visit the center*—Pay an unscheduled visit to your child's care site. Look for indications of the problem. If you can't spare the time from work, send someone you trust: a good friend, neighbor, or a relative.

- *Speak to your caregiver*—Ask for an account of what happened. This may get to the bottom of it right away. Most problems of this kind are not easily defined and don't necessarily require assigning blame. A straightforward talk may be all that's necessary.

- *Terminate the agreement*—If you feel that your baby is being poorly cared for, neglected, or abused, you must end the arrangement immediately. Don't brush off warning signs because you can't believe them or you're too busy at work to begin the caregiver search all over again. Your community agency for children's rights will tell you how to proceed if, indeed, you feel a crime has been committed.

Preventing Sexual Abuse

Several shocking stories have surfaced over the years regarding sexual abuse of children in child-care centers. Fortunately, these incidents are rare, but even one is too many.

Learn to recognize the signs of sexual abuse. Call your pediatrician immediately if you notice any of these symptoms:

- Loss of appetite or any extreme change of behavior

• Frequent nightmares, disturbed sleep, or sudden fear of the dark

• New fear of objects, people, or places

• Bed-wetting

• Thumb sucking or unusual crying

• Torn or stained underclothes

• Vaginal or rectal bleeding

• Reddened or swollen genitals or painful itching

• Precocious or sensual expressions of affection

• Sudden fear or dislike of a caregiver or a child-care site

Speak to other parents from the child-care site to see if their children are showing any of these signs and report the site to the police if necessary.

Chapter 14

What to Do If Your Child Is Sick or Injured

Of all the juggling acts a working mother must perform, taking care of a sick child has to be one of the most difficult. Once you've chosen a competent, compassionate caregiver, however, at least you can feel assured that your baby is getting the best of care, even if you can't be there.

You may find it difficult to leave a sick infant, but your baby will learn in time that separation is a part of life, and you will learn to accept this fact without guilt. In the meantime, start making contingency plans for every possibility you can think of, and when illness strikes:

- Be loving and reassuring to your child. If you're feeling anxious, try not to show it.

- Explain to an older baby what will happen during the day.

- Give your caregiver detailed instructions about treatment, medication, and food. Explain that you are to be called first in case the situation worsens and that you will call the doctor. (If you know the caregiver well and have confidence in her communication skills, you might let her call.)

- Own a comprehensive medical manual, such as the *American Academy of Pediatric's Caring for Your Baby and Young Child: Birth to Age Three.* Many minor childhood illness and ailments can be recognized and treated by referring to such a guide.

Making Sick-Care Arrangements

Discuss general safety and emergency procedures in advance with your caregiver. In case of danger, for instance, a fire, tell her to get out the house at once and phone for help from a neighbor's house. To be prepared for an injury or sudden illness, you and your caregiver must know the location of the preferred health facilities and the most direct route. If your caregiver doesn't have a car, make sure she knows what taxi service to call and always leave money for the unexpected.

Ask your pediatrician which facility provides the best child care. An emergency department that regularly treats children will have child-size equipment, such as smaller oxygen masks, and will have a staff that understands the emotional needs of children. To be sure you're ready for an emergency do the following:

1. Write down detailed instructions—Have written instructions ready for every eventuality. Don't wait until your baby falls ill in the middle of the night and then try to instruct someone in the morning when you're suffering from lack of sleep and anxiety about your baby. The instructions list should include:

- The comforting methods that work best with your baby

- Your baby's favorite books and toys

- Important telephone numbers like work numbers for you and your partner, neighbors, family members, etc.

- Ambulance company

- Poison information center

- Emergency room

- Backup person

- Local pharmacy

- Baby doctor or an in-house call service

- The conditions under which you must be called; if for example, there is a significant rise in temperature or a sign of great distress. (See "Illnesses and Injury Observation Worksheet," page 278. This will help you chart when your baby's symptoms started, how his temperature fluctuated, behavior change, etc.)

- A consent form (see "Consent for Emergency Medical Care" form, page 282). Unless the situation is life-threatening, physicians will not treat a child without parental permission.

- Diagrams of emergency shutoff valves: water, gas, etc. Paint them red.

- Directions to the hospital and telephone number of a reliable taxi service.

- The location of emergency supplies: flashlights, candles, replacement fuses, etc.

- An emergency-room information kit, including:

  - Your insurance card

  - Two lists concerning medications—one listing your baby's current medications, and one giving the medications to which your baby is allergic. Include the doses of commonly used medications for caregiver's information.

- Age and weight

- Immunization dates

- A record of health problems and illnesses

- The location of medical and first-aid supplies—Keep medications, paper cups, and other sickroom supplies in a container, such as a shoe box, to give to your caretaker for easy and sanitary access. If your child attends a child-care facility, all medication must be in the original container and properly labeled.

- A description of life-saving techniques.

- A description of CPR techniques (your local Red Cross has a wall chart). Have your child-care provider take CPR courses offered by many hospitals.

2. Have a backup ready—Last-minute emergency strategizing is stressful. Remember that caregivers get sick too, so always have a backup plan you can rely on: Ask your spouse, a friend, a family member, an on-call baby-sitter, or a nursing service to fill in.

- If your child's care facility or family home does not accept mildly ill children, your local hospital may provide sick-care programs during the day within the hospital or another site, as well as homemaker services. These insured and bonded workers usually charge by the hour with a stated minimum number of hours and will do some sickroom care and light housekeeping, such as laundry.

This type of arrangement is preferable to moving a sick baby to some strange place. You must register in advance for these programs. Ask your employer if the company subsidizes all or some of the costs of these emergency child-care programs. If so, find out how much notice you'll have to give. Try contacting your local child-care resource-and-referral agency, state-licensing agency, or pediatrician for names of other programs located nearby.

Because public-health experts and many pediatricians have acknowledged that other children have already been exposed by the time cold symptoms and other simple respiratory illnesses appear, you may wish to try to persuade your regular day-care provider to accept mildly ill children. The only changes required would be the addition of extra staff, their training, and a "quiet space" to accommodate any under-the-weather children.

3. Planning at work—You should expect to face the problem of caring for your sick child at least five times a year. Unfortunately, no U.S. workers enjoy extra paid time off to care for their sick children at the present time. Although most employees are discouraged from using their own sick or vacation leave for a child's illness, many do.

If your employer allows you to stay home for an emergency, discuss all the details in advance with your supervisor: The procedures that will be followed; the person who will take over your responsibilities; the coworker you'll contact from home, and so forth. Ask if you may take work home to do when time allows. This will indicate that you take your responsibilities seriously. If your employer allows you to bring your child to work with you, bring along her favorite toys. She'll be kept occupied, and you can spend time together and save on a baby-sitter.

4. Change the policy—If your employer won't let you take time off from work to attend to your sick child, ask him or her to consider instituting flexible, mutually acceptable, family-leave policies. The best way to attempt to change your boss's mind is to figure out all angles first.

Begin by discussing the issue with coworkers who are also parents, so you can present a united front. Then examine the sick-care options. Make a list of the local sick-child centers, and in-home caregivers. If there's a college in your town, your group may want to build a network of students who might be available on short notice.

Figure out how coworkers will handle their workload if they do need to stay home. Which coworkers might be willing to take over urgent tasks at work? Reassure your boss that you will make every effort to be available by phone.

Once you've developed a plan, schedule a meeting with the boss. Introduce the topic as a business issue, one that he'll feel compelled to address. Remind him that by making it acceptable to use your sick days to care for a sick child, both management and employees benefit. Ask him to consider lining up day-care providers for its employees when their kids are ill or ask for employee vouchers to cover the part of care-related services or add "family illness days" to their usual allotment of paid time off.

Let your employer know that it makes dollars and sense to provide new solutions to the sick-child dilemma because what he or she loses in days off will be more than made up in employee satisfaction, productivity, and loyalty. Mention that nationwide, companies lose about $3 billion a year because of absenteeism due to child-care emergencies. You have to help build the conviction in your work place that caring for a sick child is inevitable and a reasonable request so that you won't have to resort to lying about why you're staying home.

Calling the Doctor from Work

While you're on the phone with the caregiver, and before you call the doctor, ask about these signs and when they first began:

- Temperature

- Appetite

- Diarrhea

- Coughing

- Nausea/vomiting

- Rash

- Cold/stuffiness

- Constipation

- Appearance

- Breathing

- Activity level

- Swollen glands

You should always call the doctor right away if your child's fever creeps too high—100.2 degrees for babies up to three months old; 101 degrees for those three to six months old; and 103 degrees for those six months and older, or if any symptom is particularly unusual or severe.

Keep copies of the Illness Observation List at your office and at home so that you and your caregiver have information at your fingertips whenever it's needed.

Nowadays, most pediatricians have an answering service and carry beepers wherever they go. They've become experts at sorting out the need for urgent care from the mild illness that can be prescribed for over the phone. This is a blessing for the working woman with limited time. To make each call to the doctor as productive as possible, develop a plan of action with your employer and your caregiver so that everyone knows what to expect and then follow this system:

1. Write down everything you need to discuss—Before you call, spend a few minutes gathering your thoughts. Jot down your questions so you won't forget anything. In case the doctor has to call for a prescription, have the number of a convenient drug store handy.

2. Give clear, detailed information—Tell the nurse your baby's name, age, weight, symptoms, and how long they've been apparent. Temperature will vary depending on the type of thermometer you use, so be sure to tell your healthcare provider how the temperature was taken. (If your caregiver is fluent in English, it might be better for her to give the information about your baby's symptoms directly to the doctor. Relayed data can sometimes lead to miscommunication.)

A new mother will not have had experience with an ill baby and may be overly concerned. The doctor and nurse should understand this and be patient and understanding. Explain that it's important to know whether you'll have to take time off from work. The nurse may even be able to give you instructions without transferring you to the doctor when it's understood that your work complicates the situation.

3. Call during the day—If it's possible, call the doctor's office during the day when your baby's records will be immediately available, although you shouldn't hesitate to call at any time when you feel there might be a serious problem. Try not to call right before you go into a conference. If your doctor calls you back, you won't be available to receive his call.

4. Offer evidence—If possible, make a tape recording of your baby's crying and play it for the doctor over the phone or have your caregiver hold the phone close to your baby. Offer to bring a sample of your baby's stool or vomit if it would help make a diagnosis.

5. Call 911 or an ambulance—If the situation is so severe that your pediatrician tells you to call an ambulance, make sure that you clearly tell the ambulance service your name, the address of your home or child-care facility, and your phone number at work. Give the ambulance service clear directions to the place where your baby is located.

ILLNESS AND INJURY OBSERVATION WORKSHEET

Baby's most recent weight _____

Chronic health problems _____

_____

Current medications _____

_____

Doctor's name and number _____

_____

Pharmacy name and number _____

_____

Observations

1st Day/Time _____

_____

2nd Day/Time _____

_____

3rd Day/Time _____

_____

4th Day/Time _____

_____

Treatments _____

Doctor's recommendations _____

_____

EMERGENCY INFORMATION SHEET

(Place this near your telephone)

Mother's name _____ Work Phone _____

Father's name _____ Work Phone _____

Home address _____ Home Phone _____

Neighbor(s)_____ Telephone _____

Nearest Relative(s) _____ Telephone _____

Other people authorized to pick up child _____

Telephone _____

Baby-sitter/caregiver's phone_____

Police phone _____

Fire phone _____

Ambulance phone _____

Baby doctor's name_____

Partner's name_____

Office phone (weekdays)_____

(nights and weekends) _____

Hospital address_____ Phone _____

Pharmacy address_____ Phone _____

Poison control center phone_____

Taxi _____

Baby's allergies _____

Special health conditions _____

_____

Medications _____

House instructions (turn off/on gas/heat, air conditioner, security alarm, etc.)

Other information _____

_____

Baby usually eats

_____ ozs. at _____ a.m./p.m.

_____ ozs. at _____ a.m./p.m.

_____ ozs. at _____ a.m./p.m.

Feeding instructions:

_____

_____

_____

In order for someone else to secure medical care for your child, he must have your permission. You can grant this permission by signing the medical release form on the following page. Make photocopies, fill them out, then sign them, and give one to each person who takes care of your child. Keep one attached to the Emergency Information Sheet. (Note: Not all medical facilities will accept this form; some hospitals/doctors require their own release be completed.)

CONSENT FOR EMERGENCY MEDICAL CARE

I, _____

    (Mother/Father/Legal Guardian)

Hereby give my consent to _____

                (Caregiver/Day-Care Center)

Who will be caring for my child

_____

    (Name)   (Birth Date)   (Social Security No.)

For the period _____ to _____ to arrange for emergency medical/surgical/dental care and treatment (including diagnostic procedures) necessary to preserve the health of my child.

Print name: _____ Pediatrician: _____

Address: _____ Address: _____

Home phone: _____ Phone: _____

Business phone: _____ Child's allergies, if any: _____

Chronic illnesses, if any: _____

Medicines child is taking: _____

Date of last tetanus booster: _____

Name and address of primary health insurance carrier: _____

Policy no.: _____

Group no.: _____

Signature: _____

    (Mother, Father, or Legal Guardian)   (Date)

Going to the Doctor's Office

If you need to leave work and take your baby to see the doctor, win the waiting game. Some delays are inevitable, but here are ways to at least weather any long waits:

• If possible, schedule the appointment selectively. The first patient scheduled for each shift—morning, afternoon, and possibly evening, stands the best chance of being seen on time.

• Call ahead to see if the doctor is running late, so you can adjust your appointment.

• Come prepared. Dress your baby comfortably and take along a favorite "comforter," such as a pacifier, blanket, or toy. Go over the "Illness and Injury Observation Checklist" to make sure you don't forget anything. Mention any medication your caregiver has given your baby. If your caregiver will be bringing your baby, make sure she takes the "Consent for Emergency Medical Care."

• Make sure you understand the instructions for any medication, and give your written notes to your caregiver. Or make sure your caregiver gets the information from the doctor. To save waiting time, ask the doctor to phone the pharmacy with your prescription as you're leaving his office.

If the doctor cuts you short, remind him that this problem may be common in a doctor's office, but you're seeing it for the first time and you want all the information available. Never hesitate to ask questions of a professional.

Choosing a Pharmacy

To begin with, you're going to choose a pharmacy that's convenient and affordable (large chain stores often are able to lower prices because they buy at a bulk rate). In addition, look for these benefits:

• Discounts

• Free delivery

• Computerized patient profiles

• After-hours emergency services

• Accessible pharmacist to answer questions

• No insurance carrier conflicts

Part Four

Returning to Work

Chapter 15

Experiencing a Good Physical and Emotional Postpartum Recovery

The job of a working mother may be the most difficult, yet the most exciting, of your life. The challenge will begin as soon as you're home from the hospital. One minute you're in charge of your life, dressing up every day and going where you please and when; the next minute you're isolated at home with a new baby calling all the shots.

If you, and others close to you, understand what to expect, you'll be better able to deal with the physical changes and the emotional roller coaster ride of new motherhood. You can expect most of the recovery to take place within the first few days after birth, but some adjustments take place gradually over a four-to-eight week period. With the support of the important people in your life, you'll adjust to your new position and quickly take up the reins of mothering and career.

Recognizing and Dealing with Common Problems

Fatigue

First, you're in a weakened physical state, and then you have the taxing job of caring for a newborn, which gives you no time to sleep. No wonder you're tired! You may feel that you're not as competent as you were, or that you'll never again have time for yourself. But this, too, will pass. Just keep these things in mind, and you'll avoid "New Working Mom Burnout:"

• Don't try to do it all. Get help if you possibly can.

• Make the most of your time.

• Take good care of yourself. Eat well and get plenty of rest.

Baby Blues

Over 80 percent of new moms have this dispirited feeling. It shows itself in strange ways: For no obvious reason you may feel angry with your baby, your partner, or even a coworker. Unexpected crying is one symptom; others may be sleeping or eating problems or difficulty making decisions when you return to work. Routine responsibilities may seem overwhelming.

It helps to know that these common emotional extremes are caused to a large extent by hormonal changes taking place in your body. Sleep deprivation plus the natural let-down from the emotional "high" of childbirth also play a part. These feelings will pass, but in the meantime, here are some tips for getting though the rough parts:

- *Remind yourself*—Even when you know these swings are temporary, you have to keep reminding yourself of this fact. Once you express and accept these feelings, it will be easier to deal with them.

- *Rest*—Get enough sleep and rest whenever you can. Try to rest when your baby sleeps. Proper rest strengthens the immune system and helps repair damage. Don't be shy about seeking relief from mothering. Every good parent needs down time. After you're back at work, try to find a quiet time each day—say, at lunch time—just to close your eyes and rest. Don't forget to eat well and exercise gently.

- *Avoid stress*—Stay away from making life changes, such as changing jobs. Consider hiring outside help if you need it and can afford it. Ask yourself, "Can someone else do this?" Try not to let things overwhelm you. Set priorities, and the important things will get done. If coworkers, friends, or family ask to help, let them!

- *Be firm*—You can't please everyone. Listen to friendly advice, accept what works, discard what doesn't, and then find your own way of doing things. And don't apologize for doing it your way.

- *Share*—Talk to your partner or to a close and trusted coworker or friend about how you feel. Talk to someone who has experienced the same problem. Join a support group.

- *Write it down*—Keep a journal and write anything you're feeling without fear of interruption, contradiction, ridicule, or reprisal.

Postpartum Depression: A Serious State

There is an anxiety state that lasts longer and is more intense than the more common baby blues. Postpartum depression, which strikes between 10–20 percent of new mothers, may actually begin during pregnancy and not necessarily after a woman gives birth, as many doctors once thought.

It's important that this depression be recognized and treated before it gets worse. Symptoms include restlessness, memory loss, inability to concentrate, anxiety, panic attacks, compulsive behavior, insomnia, an inability to cope despite adequate rest and recuperation, hallucinations, and a feeling that you might harm (or you do harm) the baby. If you experience feelings of intense sadness, anxiety, or despair that interfere with your ability to function:

- *Consult your doctor*—Your obstetrician will assess your condition and may send you to a psychiatrist or other therapist, or prescribe medication if necessary.

- *Before your appointment*—Write down your symptoms and consider taking someone with you for support.

• *Look for professional support*—For information regarding support groups for postpartum depression, contact www.WebMD.org.

Body Adjustments

During the six-week postpartum period, your body will be:

• Losing from fifteen to twenty pounds in weight, including about four pounds of fluid

• Decreasing blood volume by one-third

• Normalizing hormone levels, urinary function, and intestinal function

• Repairing tears, stitches, strained muscles, and stretched tissues

All of these changes will cause general body aches, leaking breasts, and heavy lochia flow. In addition, you may feel burning, pain, or itching from the episiotomy.

Warning Signs

After delivery, most women are very aware of their bodies. You'll notice the normal changes. But also be alert for abnormal changes. Call your doctor—don't wait for the six-week checkup—if any of the following occur:

- Fever over 100 degrees

- Painful or burning urination, urgency (sudden, strong desire to urinate), and unusual frequency

- Heavier-than-normal bleeding

- Vaginal discharge with peculiar color or odor

- Pain, swelling, or tenderness in legs, chest, or lower abdomen

- Chest pain and cough

- Hot, tender, or bleeding breasts

- Persistent perineal pain with increasing tenderness

What to Expect at Your Six-Week Checkup

It's routine for your doctor to examine you five or six weeks following the birth of your baby. Come prepared with all your questions; discuss anything that concerns you. The examination should include a check of the following:

- Blood pressure and weight

- Breasts and stomach

• Urine

• Size, shape, and location of uterus and bladder

• Vagina and cervix

• Episiotomy, lacerations, or Caesarean incision

• Hemorrhoids and varicose veins

• Pap test

Menstrual Period

Normally, your regular menstrual period will return in seven to nine weeks. If you're breast-feeding, it may not return for several months or until you've weaned your baby. There may be some irregularity in your cycle at first, but gradually it will return to normal. Be aware that your ovaries may begin to function before your regular period starts, whether you're breast-feeding or not.

If you do not want to conceive another child right away, begin contraception as soon as you resume intercourse. Ask your doctor to suggest a safe type of contraceptive for your needs. (If you don't want to have another baby, your partner may want to consider having a vasectomy. Nowadays, it's only a ten minute, non-evasive, relatively pain-free, out-patient procedure.)

Sex and the Working Mother

Decrease in sexual desire is a common complaint among new mothers. It's as though Nature makes sure that mothers will concentrate their energies on their newborns. On the other hand, your spouse may feel rejected if he doesn't understand this normal development. It's a potentially rocky period, which may be avoided by talking about feelings honestly and understanding that your lack of desire is only temporary.

Postnatal Health Tips

As you prepare to reenter the workforce, remember that the first rule of postnatal care is: be good to yourself. Whether there's a crisis at work or you've had a sleepless night—after the care of the baby—you come first. Follow these general rules, and you'll soon be feeling like your old self again:

- *Drink fluids*—You need at least two quarts a day to replenish moisture loss through hormone imbalance and milk production.

- *Relax*—When time permits, or during breaks, or at lunch time, sit in a comfortable chair, turn on soft music, and practice relaxation breathing.

- *Nurture yourself*—Set aside time for yourself. Don't feel that every evening and weekend must be spent doing something practical and productive.

Chapter 16

Overcoming Back-to-Work Anxieties

Problem solving has always come naturally to you as a working woman. It should be no different with the common worries of most working mothers. There are solutions! Just understand what to expect, find support for your concerns at home and at work, and you'll learn to overcome your anxieties.

Answers to the Most Common Worries of Working Mothers

Here are the five concerns most often expressed by working mothers and some tips to help alleviate them:

1. *You won't bond with your baby*—You worry that you've returned to work before you've bonded with your child. There's no evidence to suggest that an early return will affect your baby's normal development. Bonding isn't glue. It comes through interactions during the typical child-care activities over months and years.

2. *Your caregiver will be closer to your baby than you*—You wouldn't be human if you didn't feel competitive with your care provider. Of course, you want both your child and caregiver to love each another—but not too much. If you work at it, you can learn to respect your caregiver for the skill and interest she brings to the job without viewing this interloper as some kind of rival. Studies show that the strongest emotional bonds are between a mother and her child, regardless of who supplements the care.

   If you begin to feel jealous of your child's attachment to the caregiver, stop to realize that this doesn't mean any loss of love for you. In fact, it means just the opposite. Your child may be so overcome with love for you, and with the fear that you would leave, that she clings to the caregiver. Besides, the more people who love your baby, the more special and secure your baby will feel.

   Understandably, it hurts you to know that your care provider, not you, will see your child's first step. But take some comfort in knowing that when your baby smiles at you for the first time it will be a special moment. And when you hear the first recognizable word, the thrill will be just as great. For now, you have to focus on your need for a loving caregiver.

3. *Absence from home*—Be honest and realistic about the demands and priorities of your life. Understand that the unrealistic expectations of others come from outdated views of what a woman's role in society should be. Remember that you love your work, that you need the challenge it provides, and that your child is not suffering but is receiving excellent care.

Think of yourself as your child's role model for achievement and feelings of self-worth. Remember that mothers who stay home have their own guilt because they're not contributing to the family income, and they sometimes resent their lack of freedom. Make up for your absence by phoning several times a day and schedule a play/talk time every evening.

4. *You will spoil your baby*—Continue to lavish love and affection on your baby. There is no more important contribution you can make to your child's well-being than to help develop a sense of self-worth and of being lovable. After all, a loving, stable environment is just what your baby needs. On the other hand, if you cling to your child, it will interfere with the development of a self-reliant, independent individual.

5. *You will snap at your child*—Perhaps you're preoccupied with thoughts of work when your child intrudes and you show your irritation. Explain to your child that you're tense, or worried, or tired—and apologize for your quick temper. Force yourself to clear your mind of work concerns and give undivided attention to your child.

How to Prevent "Super Working-Mother Syndrome"

The "Super Working-Mother Syndrome" is a major trap that many working mothers fall into. In order to protect their families from the physical, mental, and social effects of their return to the workplace, many women feel compelled to "overload" their lives by doing too much in too little time. This trend for perfectionism is driven by guilt and anger. The maternal guilt basically comes from not living up to your own expectations of yourself, and the anger comes from having to self-sacrifice all day long, week in and week out.

It is important that you get past these destructive attitudes and projections. Try to dispel the notion that you can, and should, do everything perfectly: be a perfect mother, a perfect wife, and a perfect employee. It's not humanly possible. Until you acknowledge to yourself that it's okay to be less than perfect at everything, you'll carry a heavy burden of tension, a feeling of inadequacy, and disappointment. Being a balanced woman is an ongoing process—it is not a destination.

Here is a list to help you rid yourself of the symptoms before they lead to frustration, and eventually, depression:

- *Learn to recognize "warning signs"*—Physical symptoms, irritability, yelling, tears, etc., may indicate you need (and deserve) emotional sustenance. Accept the validity of what you're feeling, of the fact that you have needs that must be met if you are to function as a working mom.

- *Alter your expectations*—Ask yourself whether they are realistic and try to come to terms with them. Constantly remind yourself that you can't be all things to all people. Make a list of every last thing you feel bad about that you didn't do for your child. Feel really awful about all of them for a day, then ask forgiveness of yourself and sweep them away. Tomorrow is another day.

- *Understand that guilt comes with the territory*—Use it as a motivating force to do something positive; for example, find the best child care available. Make sure you're not projecting your own feelings of guilt and frustration on your child or she will start believing that everything is her fault, and she is the cause of your grief. Let negative comments go in one ear and out the other.

- *Become a happy, fulfilled person*—Somebody who is taking care of her own needs. This is the most important thing you can do to promote your child's future welfare. Engage in any worthwhile activity that brings you a sense of satisfaction.

- *Separate your feelings from your actions*—Feeling like hitting your child is not something to feel guilty about; hitting your child is.

- *Set priorities*—Decide which are most important to you and which you can live without. These can be tough choices, but not making them deprives you of the time you need to really enjoy your life. Once you've set your priorities, don't add a new activity unless you subtract one.

- *Slow down at work and at home*—You don't have to be number one in your department or have the cleanest house on the block. Drop the fantasy that you can come home after an easy day's work and bake delicious cookies for the family. Give them store-bought ones. Your family will love you just the same, and you'll be more fun to be around.

Learn to delegate chores you loathe or pay someone to do them. (see "Organizing Your Life to Meet the Needs of Work," page 315).

• *Seek counseling*—If you feel your life is unmanageable, a therapist can help you put things into the proper perspective and enable you to find balance in your life. If you're single, find a good support group. Your insurance company can be a good place to start. Many feature a variety of self-improvement programs at no cost to you. Your local library is another great place for info on support groups in your area as well as searching the Internet. Your local church or synagogue may also have a group that would be the right fit for you.

BACK-TO-WORK TIPS

Soon after Your Baby is Born

- Call a good friend in the office. He or she can share all the birth and baby details with everyone.
- Call the office from time to time. Your objective is to keep in touch. Unless you've structured your maternity leave to include office work, keep shop talk out of the conversation. Be polite, but steer the conversation to other subjects.
- Be definite about your return date.

Four Weeks before

- Complete your child-care arrangements.
- Make emergency sick-care arrangements (see page 268).

Three Weeks before

- Take stock of your wardrobe. If you gained weight, as most women do, don't rely on squeezing into old clothes or wearing maternity clothes back to work. You want to look your best, so buy a few pieces that fit your post-baby body or borrow from a friend. Some maternity things can be used; for instance, you can belt a jumper. Or take your maternity things to a consignment shop and buy new clothes with the proceeds.
- Talk to your hairdresser. Have your hair done in a style that's easy to maintain. You won't have the time for elaborate preparations before work.

Two Weeks before

- Contact the office again. Get an update on what's happening to the business, and ask to have industry reports or trade journals sent to you.

- Eliminate guesswork. Make sure your household and baby-care routines have been well established so that any problems are eliminated and stress is minimized.

One Week before

- Show off your baby. Stop in at the office for a short visit to let your associates meet your baby (see "Taking Your Baby to Meet Your Coworkers," page 306).
- Stop in at the office by yourself. Straighten up your desk and go through papers that might have accumulated. You might take some paperwork home to give you a head start on resuming your duties. At the very least, call your boss to check on the current state of projects and to say how you're looking forward to coming back.
- Try a couple of trial runs away from your baby. These will prevent you from being emotionally overwhelmed on your first day at work. In addition, you'll be able to test your child-care arrangement and make sure that your estimated travel time to work has been figured properly.
- Ask your caregiver to stop by. Talk about your baby's routine and clear up any confusions or misunderstandings. Prepare the list of emergency numbers.

First Day Back

- Start midweek. It's preferable to return to work sometime in the middle of the week, rather than on Monday, because then your first week is shorter than usual, and you won't be as tired.
- Feed your baby before leaving. That way your caregiver can concentrate on watching and playing with your baby rather than on feeding her. Also, if your baby is upset about your leaving, she may refuse to eat throughout the day.
- Don't socialize at first. Don't plan lunches or any social activity after work for the first few days in order to save energy. If there are social functions that

don't interfere with your getting home on time, be sure to attend, at least long enough to chat with coworkers.

- Hit the ground running. Try to arrive half an hour early the first day wearing your most professional-looking outfit. Make your entrance as a businesswoman who is still in business.

- Set up meetings with key people, including clients, your boss, your staff, and other company players. Use these meetings to refresh your insight on current projects, familiarize yourself with new projects, or get a glimpse of projects that may be coming down the pipeline in the near future. You'll be letting everyone know that you're back 100 percent.

- Remain businesslike. Keep the talk about your baby and childbirth to a minimum. Make your first day back at work as productive as ever.

- Be prepared for changes. Even when you've been briefed, there will be moments when you'll feel out of touch. It'll take time to settle in and feel in control again. Don't let mixed feelings get the best of you.

- Check with home unobtrusively. At first, you'll probably make many calls to reassure yourself that everything is well at home. Do it quickly when no one else is around.

- Reassure your boss. You want your employer to feel that you're at ease about your child care and that it won't interfere with your performance at work.

Helping Your Baby and Yourself with Separation Anxiety

Before the age of five months, babies usually don't show signs of distress when they're separated from their parents. From that time until about five years of age, however, if you notice any of the following signs, it indicates that your baby may be feeling separation anxiety:

- Increasing wariness and fear of strangers

- Increasing distress when you leave

- Clinging to you

- Crying inconsolably with a sitter

Dos and Don'ts for Dealing with Baby's Fears

There are several ways to approach your baby's separation anxiety to make it easier on everyone:

- Do choose a time when your baby is usually alert and happy to introduce a new caregiver. Never begin a potentially stressful encounter when your baby is sick or cranky.

- Do reassure your child by using a positive tone of voice to explain what's going to occur. Even a baby understands a calm voice. Treat any stranger entering your home in a welcoming way to show that you have no anxiety. You show that you're to be trusted and relied upon more by your actions than by words. Always be truthful about where you're going and when you're returning. Confidence will build when it's clear you're trustworthy.

- Do arrange some time for a new caregiver and your baby to become acquainted. Insist that the same routine and pattern of child rearing be maintained. Keep photos of yourself around so your caregiver can point at the pictures and talk about how Mommy will be back soon.

- Do play quiet games before the encounter to keep your child peaceful—no running around. A quieter child will find it easier to say goodbye. You can help your baby understand this process of separation by playing peek-a-boo. This game demonstrates that while Mommy may disappear for a while, she'll reappear.

- Do give your baby a "lovey" to hold: a favorite plush animal or a security blanket. These help your baby to cope with his fears and frustrations.

- Do give your baby time to readjust to you when you return. Talk affectionately, but keep your distance until your baby is ready to come to you. Your baby needs to learn that even when she has these feelings, you're ready to help overcome the sense of discomfort.

- Don't rush when your baby is crying and pulling at you. Keep talking and holding your baby lovingly.

- Don't worry if your baby is upset. All babies go through this period. It actually represents a developmental step forward because it shows recognition that you two are separate people.

- Don't be scornful of your child's feelings. Always be sympathetic and supportive, but do your best not to be overprotective. That would curb an adventurous spirit and weaken self-confidence.

- Don't ever force your child to go to a stranger.

Reducing Your Own Fears

- *You grieve when you leave home*—These feelings are perfectly normal. Accept some self-doubt and sadness—it's part of the trade-off. You'll learn to gradually accept the distance between you and your child and to cherish your time together at the end of the day.

- *Express your feelings*—Tell your child about the sense of loss and loneliness you feel. You'll probably be putting into words the same emotions your child feels.

- *Talk to others*—Other mothers will understand how you feel, and perhaps have some tips to help you get through the day.

- *Locate a child-care center closer to your work*—With child care close to your office, you can stroll over and observe that your child is doing well. You can even go to lunch together occasionally, if you think it won't upset your child to go through yet another parting.

- *Take time off*—Take an occasional afternoon off to be with your baby. Both of you will look forward to these days.

Taking Your Baby to Meet Your Coworkers

Quality time is for the enjoyment of both child and parent. But a special treat for a mother is to show her baby to the people at work. So plan to stop by the office for a short visit before your maternity leave is over. The best time to visit is during a coffee break. Be sure you take these precautions:

- *Call ahead to get your supervisor's permission*—Mention that your visit will be short.

- *Call to see if anyone in the office is sick or has been exposed to disease*—Remember that a baby, especially in the first three months, doesn't have a fully functioning immune system.

- *Bring a fully stocked diaper bag.*

- *Dress your baby in layers, rather than in heavy garments*—Protect the baby's clothes with a bib until you get there. Remove the outer garments once you're there to avoid getting your baby overheated.

- *If you don't feel up to bringing your baby to work, have work come to you*—Invite people at times that avoid you having to cook a meal for them. Pace your visits. See them only when you want to.

Controlling Stress and Becoming a Contented Working Parent

The kind of pressured existence that working parents live can rob everyone of the opportunity to enjoy life together. What is worse, so much stress can make us irritable, and that has a corrosive effect on families. The following suggestions will be reminders from time to time of the kind of parent you want to be:

1. *Approach your challenges with a sense of joy*—You'll find the first few weeks after childbirth much easier to deal with if you keep this in mind. Celebrate your victories and remember them on days when you feel like a failure.

2. *Accentuate the positive*—Some days will be difficult if not downright infuriating. On those days, try to think of the positive side of motherhood. Focus on the many wonderful things about your child. Keep

funny or endearing photos in your wallet. Look at them when you're having dark thoughts at work.

3. *Seize spontaneous moments to play with your child*—A short play period with your baby after you get home from the office is a great way to release tensions and irritations. Children treasure many experiences that don't take much time or don't need to be scheduled.

4. *Focus on your child when you're together*—Don't get into the habit of thinking about something else when you're with your child. Requests will begin to feel like interruptions, and your child's very presence may feel like an intrusion. Once you're at home, put away the problems of the workplace. If you have trouble controlling your thoughts, put your concerns on a piece of paper, put it in an envelope, and seal it. Tell yourself you won't think about it until the envelope is opened.

5. *Accept your own decisions about your child*—If you worry every time you make a decision concerning your child, you'll be under unnecessary stress. You can't be right about everything you do. Make your best decision, and if it's wrong, make another one to correct it.

6. *Schedule your own needs*—Take the time to discover what refreshes you and makes you feel good about yourself. Nurture your body and soul with things like reading, napping, painting, bathing, cooking, or

writing. You will be amazed by how much energy and patience you will have after having a rendezvous with yourself for one hour.

7. *Diffuse your anger*—Find ways to avoid the angry moment. If your child starts crying when you pick up the telephone, save your call until nap time. Give yourself a time out when your toddler is driving you up the wall. Put your child in a safe place, then go into another room. Breathe deeply, count to ten, and hit a pillow. Do whatever you need to do to safely release your anger.

8. *Be a good role model*—You have the chance to teach your child how to handle stress by your example. In the long run, this will make parenting much easier. Take things in stride, be patient, keep a realistic perspective, and set a good precedent.

9. *Get support*—Everyone around you, at home and at work, may be good resources for information, advice, and help with your child. Don't hesitate to ask for help. Also, look for a nearby parenting center, or a mother's support group off- or online to help you through bad times.

Options to Consider When Your Job and Motherhood Don't Mix

As much as you love your job, you may find that your present career and motherhood are not compatible. Before you make a move, though, consider the benefits you might be losing. It's hard to provide health care for a child, for example, without medical insurance. Make sure you have enough cash on hand to get the family through a period without your income. In other words, there are risks involved.

Choosing a New Occupation

When you're exploring career options, keep your search focused. Limit your interest to no more than the three areas that most appeal to you. The easiest way to change a career is to choose something that builds on your past experience. For example, a medically trained person could look in the health-insurance field where they need people to analyze claims. The following steps are essential:

1. *Assess your skills*—The most expensive option for this test—but the one that guarantees expert advice—is a career counselor. Personal recommendations are the best way to find a good one. Lacking that, you could ask a psychologist, a psychiatrist, or other professional association. Other sources would be:

   • Outplacement firms
   • College career-development offices
   • American Society for Training and Development
   • Community college career-counseling service
   • University alumni clubs' counseling services

2. *Test new possibilities*—Some occupations look more attractive from afar than they really are. You can't go back to school full-time to test a career's potential. But you can test the water with your toe by taking a few evening classes. Another way is to moonlight on the side to examine the culture of your prospective industry, or perhaps, take a temporary job during your vacation.

3. *Consider the cost*—Gone are the days when you could throw caution to the winds and make changes impulsively. Now you have a family's security to think about. Your first task is to consider the affordability of the proposed career change. The standard advice to job changers is to have adequate cash on hand to cover family expenses for several months. In times of economic slowdown your cash reserve should cover at least six months. The alternative of starting your own business, an even riskier venture, requires a reserve of up to a year's expenses. Draw up a budget to pinpoint areas where expenses can be trimmed (see "Budget Strategies to Meet Your Family's Growing Needs," page 189) and be sure to pay down credit card balances; a time of austerity may be ahead.

Start Looking from Work

Ideally, your search for something new will take place while you're still working. Not only will your salary and benefits continue, but also, ironically, an applicant for a job looks more interesting to an employer when he or she is still employed elsewhere. Your search should begin with networking, and here are some ideas to do that:

- *Expand your business contacts*—Speak to customers, suppliers, lawyers, anyone you come in contact with in the course of business. Don't forget to let your accountant, your banker, and vendors know that you're in the market for a new job. Of course, if you're still employed, ask these contacts to be discreet about your new job search.

- *Use professional organizations*—Perhaps the most fruitful source of information is a professional or industry organization. The country's largest female network, the National Association for Female Executives, is an excellent source. Also, you'll find chapters of the Business and Professional Women's Association throughout the country. The list of organizations is almost endless. You can also get online or tap business message boards for support and tips.

Starting a Business

Sufficient capital is the lifeblood of any business, particularly a new one that needs some time to get established. More than 50 percent of new businesses fail within the first four years, almost always because of lack of capital. Yet, beginning entrepreneurs find it very hard to obtain borrowed money. In times of economic stress, obtaining a loan, or a grant of any size, is all but impossible, according to experts.

One source of limited help is the Federal Small Business Administration. Although funding has been reduced, the agency still guarantees some loans and recently announced plans to grant "micro" loans of up to $15,000 to new business ventures. Another source is the National Association for Female

Executives' venture-capital program. The group makes investments of between $5,000 and $50,000 to members with an association-approved business plan. Otherwise, the only other practical options are independent venture-capital funds or loans from private investors.

A home-based business is the answer for many women. Approximately two million American women currently own and operate their own home-based businesses. No more traffic jams and expensive child-care fees for them. Compared to retainer franchises, home-based franchises are easy enough to start. A business letterhead and a phone line are all that's needed. In general, they require less capital than other business ventures, and the percentage of profit is greater because there are no overhead expenses for an office or a store.

These franchises can be risky, however, because many of the products are new ideas that have no established track record. Also, you must be sure the franchise company has backup systems that you can call on when you need to. Some of the two thousand franchises available give you nothing more for your money (around $10,000) than marketing materials, a training tape, and a handshake at the door.

Starting your own business takes commitment, a solid business plan, and a support system. The American Women's Economic Development Corporation is a nonprofit origination dedicated to advising women entrepreneurs. This group and the Small Business Administration offer pamphlets, counseling, and seminars on how to start and manage a business. Use these organizations to develop a support network of the professionals you'll need later on.

Returning to School

A small amount of retraining may be feasible while you're still working. You may even get your employer to cover the costs if it relates to your present job. Attending school full time is a costly way to retrain your self. It not only requires high tuition fees but also the loss of your salary. Start out by taking individual classes that have been recommended to you by people who work in the field you aspire to enter. Some women have done it, but taking a full load at school, caring for your baby, and working full-time needs almost superhuman strength.

If you do decide to leave work for full-time education, a number of scholarships and loan programs are available to adult students. Information about and applications for several of these programs are available from the Business and Professional Women's Foundation.

Chapter 17

Organizing Your Life to Meet the Needs of Work

As a working mother you'll be juggling two jobs: your duties at home and at your job. That's a demanding schedule even when you have emotional and financial support from others.

Typically, it's inflexible job schedules that create much of the pressure on two-career families. The mutual support so necessary to a good marriage and family becomes more difficult when each partner is overextended. Because everyone has needs, they can be met successfully only by striking the right balance. The best way to deal with the stress you're under is for both of you to learn how to share the responsibilities of your busy life.

Tips for Successful Task-Sharing at Home

1. *Identify priorities*—First and foremost, you need to identify what tasks take priority and where potential sources of conflict lie. This requires both of you to know the other's schedule by using a family calendar.

The keys to success lie in keeping focused and in maintaining a balance between work life and home life.

2. *Be organized*—For working couples, organization means the difference between function and dysfunction. When you have a system, you avoid wasting precious time and energy. You accomplish more, are more effective, and live an easier life because you're more in control.

3. *Keep communication open*—Try to keep a constant flow of communication between you, even when busy schedules make that very difficult. Communication is a learned skill. Practice it until it becomes second nature.

4. *Negotiate solutions*—Discuss how all the duties, baby care, and household chores will be divided. Approach the search for solutions with an open mind. Smooth negotiations are bound to lead to happy outcomes. They may not be the solutions you had expected, but the best interests of your family have been served.

5. *Be adaptable*—Not only do you need to rearrange priorities now that you're a mother, but you also need to be more adaptable than every before. For example, you both need a short period of relaxation at the end of the workday. Then the pressure of baby care and preparing dinner won't seem as great. You can't do it together, though, when a small, demanding child is around. So take turns on alternate days to

read a newspaper or catch forty winks. At least one of you will feel more relaxed every other day. Contentment will be yours when you share the load. You will have broken away from stereotyped roles and will have negotiated new ones.

6. *Remember that the tasks you're so busy "getting through" (e.g., eating, bathing, bedtime) are what memories are made of*—Become more mindful of the passing moment, instead of trying to push your kids through their days.

Ten Steps to Accomplishing Your Goals at Home

Going back to work as a new mother takes very detailed planning. To be successful both at work and at home, you need to be organized. Getting organized isn't difficult if you approach it one step at a time. Here is a step-by-step plan for keeping organized at home:

1. *Analyze the task assignments*—Think about whether you're satisfied with the way the work is shared. Work an equitable assignment of functions so that you aren't overwhelmed with the whole job after a long day at work. Eliminate unnecessary tasks and hire out others.

2. *Save time by spending a little more money*—In the long run, you have only two things to spend—time and money. If you want to save on one, you'll have to spend the other. Therefore, think seriously about buying labor-saving devices; for example, a microwave oven or a dishwasher.

3. *Keep a calendar*—Use a large wall calendar to keep track of everything on the schedule. Have a short conference each week with your partner to go over the next week's activities.

4. *Make lists*—Make a list of weekly tasks and cross them off as they're completed. You'll be surprised how well this system brings order out of chaos.

5. *Look for shortcuts*—Most chores, both at home and at work, lend themselves to shortcuts. Some jobs can be cut down; some can be done less perfectly. Do a general pick-up the night before, and the next day's house-cleaning will be more manageable. To put a twist on a popular business saying—if it ain't dirty, don't clean it.

6. *Respect differences*—You may have to teach your partner how to do some jobs. But once you've done that, stand back and allow him to do it in his own way. Be generous with praise.

7. *Work with small blocks of time*—Complete small tasks or nibble away at large jobs in small blocks of time. Learn not to be upset if you have to stop in the middle of something.

8. *Be orderly as you do each task*—Train yourself to work from left to right and top to bottom. Stand in one place while you're cleaning and do everything within reach before moving on to another position.

9. *Learn to do two things at once*—Read your baby a story while you're waiting for the wash to finish. Talk to a friend on the phone while you're cooking dinner. Plan your errands so that everything in one neighborhood is done in the same trip. Write a quick note to a friend while waiting for a client.

10. *Save time and eat well at work and home*—Shop and plan meals that will make you more efficient and increase your leisure hours.

A SAMPLE PLAN FOR HECTIC WORKDAYS

The Night Before

- *Prepare clothes*—Listen to the weather report, know what to expect, and have the proper cleaned and pressed clothes ready to go.
- *Prepare for work and day care*—Pack your briefcase and your baby's diaper bag. Keep the items you need near the door to avoid last-minute frantic searches.
- *Mix formula.*
- *Fix lunches.*
- *Plan breakfast*—Serve everyone the same breakfast to save time and dirty cooking pans.
- *Prepare the table.*
- *Prepare caregiver instructions*—Write instructions down; don't plan to depend on your memory. Keep them in your briefcase or the handbag you're planning to use the next day.

In the Morning

- *Get up earlier*—You'll be surprised what a difference in composure an hour makes. You have more time to get yourself ready and to spend with your family. What's more, you can more easily cope with the unexpected when, for example, your caregiver calls in sick or your baby spits up on your only clean blouse.

After Work

- *Use the trip home to relax*—On public transportation, take a book for relaxation and get your mind off responsibilities. Listen to soft music in your car, not the bad news of the day. Use devices such as an iPod to organize and store your personal favorite playlists consisting of calming and relaxing music you enjoy the most, or record comical stand ups from your favorite comedians to listen to wherever you go to keep yourself in a good mood. Laughter is the best relaxer.

- *Leave problems at the office*—Prepare to meet your child again. Think of positive things; take a few deep breaths and relax. The office problems will still be there in the morning when you're better able to deal with them.
- *Focus on your child*—This is a high-stress, low-energy time of day for your baby also. Be understanding if your child remembers feeling anger and confusion during your morning departure and greets you with resentment.
- *Talk things over with your caregiver*—This is the time to go over events of the day and uncover any problems. It's also an interim time for your child to adjust to your arrival.
- *Develop a good-bye ritual*—Small children find it difficult to have the continuity of their lives disrupted. A good-bye ritual will make leaving a child-care center easier. For instance, a good-bye wave to the caregiver or teacher, to a favorite toy, or another child is reassuring. Bring a special toy or treat for the ride home, such as soft fruit slices or easily digested oat cereal.

In the Evening

- *Get comfortable*—As soon as you get home, change into something comfortable. This can become a symbolic signal that it's time to stop thinking about work and to begin a family life.
- *Have a dinner planned in advance*—Plan your weekday evening meals so that they are simple and fast to make.
- *Concentrate on your child*—Plan a relaxing ritual or some activities that are done

only at this reconnecting time. Be generous with hugs and kisses. Talk about the evening ahead. In other words, make homecoming a positive experience (see "Dos and Don'ts for Quality Baby Time," page 323). Eat a high protein snack at 3 or 4 p.m. so that you have enough energy for what's ahead.

- *Save time for yourself*—If you neglect yourself, you won't have the stamina for all the things you want to do. Read, knit, surf the net; in other words, have fun!
- *Avoid struggles*—Quality time with your child has less to do with physical needs than with doing things you all enjoy. Don't butt heads over disliked foods or insist on a bath when your child doesn't want one.
- *Limit interruptions*—Let the message machine or voice mail take your calls during the evening visit with your child. Return the calls later.
- *Make dinnertime peaceful*—Set the stage for good behavior at the table. Turn off the TV, turn some quiet music on low, and make it clear that dinnertime is for pleasant conversation, not bickering.
- *Clear the table together*—This should be a cooperative effort. Even a toddler can carry a spoon to the sink.
- *Create a peaceful sleeping environment*—Help your baby go straight to sleep with the hum of a fan, sound of the dryer, ride in a car, running vacuum, or rumbling dryer.
- *Improvise*—Organizational strategies will work one week but not necessarily the next. Be ready to improvise. When life at home goes smoothly, everyone wins.

Making the Most of Time with Your Baby

While the catch phrase "quality time" means many things to many people, studies reveal that babies need be exposed to caring parental interest for only about one hour a day in order to thrive. This research proves that the length of time babies spend without their mothers counts far less than the quality of the time spent with them. Love should never be measured according to time. Love is what you put into time, no matter how little you have.

Dos and Don'ts for Quality Baby Time

Quality time doesn't have to involve elaborate entertainment. It simply means making the beginning and end of each day together something special and intimate. It's more than a spotless house, and it should come before any worries about the job. This is the time to enjoy being a parent. There are many pleasurable things you can do, and some things you should avoid, including:

- Do sing, talk softly, or hum on the way to and from child care to create an atmosphere of fun and serenity.

- Do use animated gestures when you speak, and smile often. Ask questions and make eye contact.

- Do read often to your baby. It helps language development, and it's a great opportunity for physical closeness. An infant enjoys just having pictures explained.

- Do have spontaneous play. Just get down on the floor and follow whatever your child is doing.

- Don't tune out your child. Always take your child's feelings seriously; really listen.

- Don't over program. Evening time together should be simple, relaxing, satisfying experiences. Your child doesn't expect to be constantly entertained. Stop at a park in daylight or take a short stroller ride around the block.

- Don't feel that you must give undivided attention at all times. You can continue with your activities while you're talking. Share some daily tasks when your child is old enough. For example, provide toy cookware while you're preparing dinner. Or take a bath together.

- Don't equate quality time with absence of discipline or limits.

- Don't feel guilty because your time together is not like a greeting-card commercial.

Keeping Your Marriage Fresh

Working couples who want to make their marriages work too, should make time for one another aside from all the other details of parenthood. Focus on placing your special time together high on your priority list.

Keeping the spark alive will take effort at times, but you know that the rewards will be worth it. Keep the following points in mind:

- *Reflect on what you're learning together*—To nurture your relationship and keep communication open, discuss from time to time the positive things you're learning as parents. It'll boost your self-esteem and sense of satisfaction too. At the end of a working day, don't greet each other with negative news. Wait until a quiet time when everyone is relaxed.

- *Find time for special moments*—Eliminate unproductive or repetitive activities in order to make time for yourselves. Let the clean laundry go unfolded occasionally. Pour two glasses of wine and turn the lights down low. Or ask a friend, coworker, or family member to baby sit for a couple hours so you can have a romantic getaway.

- *Set aside a problem resolution time*—Have specific blocks of time when you discuss child-related issues with your partner. Keep it separate from your fun time together as a couple.

- *Cultivate common interests*—Don't lose sight of the fact that parenthood is just one aspect of your marriage and not the whole expression. Find interests, friends, and activities you can share as a couple at least once a week. Try to get away one weekend every few months.

- *Learn to say no*—The time you save by eliminating needless tasks could be used for strengthening your marriage bonds.

- *Be thoughtful*—Send notes to each other expressing your feelings. Considerate, unexpected gifts do wonders for a relationship. Call during your lunch hour to say hello.

Accomplishing Your Goals at Work

Planning ahead and being organized are essential to your continued success on the job. The following are easy-to-follow tips for staying organized at work:

1. *Work productively*—List your tasks in advance for the week. Stay focused and start each day with your priorities in mind. Whatever isn't finished at the end of the day should be done first thing the next morning.

2. *Carry a calendar*—Divide each page in half: one side for business, and the other for home.

3. *Schedule the most demanding activities during the time of day when you have the greatest energy*—Whether it's a high-pressure sales call or attending a "Mommy & Me" class with your baby, make sure you are up for the challenge. Try to leave at least 10 percent of your schedule open each day to accommodate "emergencies" such as pulling together a last-minute presentation or taking your sick baby to the doctor.

4. *Make a master list*—Not just a "To do" list, but a list that notes every single task and appointment—from the names and numbers of people to call to the status of current work projects to taking your baby in for a doctor's appointment to dropping off dry cleaning—that will use up the time in your day. Ask yourself what is the most important thing you need to do now and do it. And then check off your list. Pinpoint the time wasters: Things you don't really need to do at all, things you can put off, things other people can do for you.

5. *Say No*—It's nice to be needed but your time is at a premium now. Recognize when and to whom you can say no and practice exercising that option as often as possible.

6. *Keep a sense of humor*—It will help you like nothing else to enjoy the good moments and weather the bad.

7. *Don't bring your baby to the office while you work on Saturdays too often*—When you do, spend some time interacting with him afterward (go for a walk, etc).

Transitioning from Work to Home

- *Prepare yourself, mentally and physically, for your arrival home*—Make a list of work tasks for your next day in order to free your mind from them. Plan ahead to finish at work that which can't wait until the next day before you leave the office. You'll be more emotionally available for your family when you're at home. Cultivate a work-free zone in your mind, so when your workday is over, your mind is free. You'll be more fun to be with, plus you'll feel more refreshed to tackle your work when you return to the office.

• *Ease your daily reunion*—Avoid coming into your child's day-care center in a big hurry. You're changing the demeanor of calm that's been established all day. You've been gone all day, and now all of a sudden you're rushing her.

• *On the ride home yield to your child's preferred style*—Some like to chat or chatter, but don't push. You might bring a light snack in the car, let your child pick the music, or talk about what's up for the evening.

• *Once through the front door, take it slow and easy*—Sudden dramatic shifts can discombobulate young children. Give at least a tiny amount of full attention to your baby right away—if he wants it. But then take care of yourself for a few minutes. Plan for a drink, a snack, checking the mail, and a brief snuggle on the couch.

• *Continue to breast-feed*—After you've returned to work, breast-feeding helps you transition from your working day to your family time.

• *Soak away stress*—Move bath time to evening transition time. Taking a bath with your baby will work wonders and free up the after-dinner hour for other activities.

- *Get casual*—Change into something comfortable when you get home so that you become a cuddly mom rather than a uptight business-woman. It will help your kids feel secure that you're in for the night. Ask your baby for help choosing your "play clothes."

- *Designate a particular activity for transition hour every day*—Set up a game, a puzzle, or a craft. Or have the whole family take a short de-stressing walk before dinner.

Chapter 18

Breast-Feeding and the Working Woman

Controversy still swirls around the issue of breast- versus bottle-feeding. If you're not sure which method to use, you can try starting with breast-feeding and switching later. Once you decide to bottle feed, however, you'll lose the breast-feeding option because your milk supply will dry up without the stimulation of your baby's sucking. Your success with breast-feeding once you return to work will depend upon your confidence with your decision, and how well you organize it.

Combining Breast-Feeding and Working

Combining breast-feeding with working takes careful planning and a determination to see it through. Remember that the demands of the job will continue in spite of your special circumstances. If you don't assume the responsibility for your feeding plan, no one else will. First, if possible, allow at least eight weeks before returning to work in order to:

- Recover from your child's birth

- Establish your milk supply

- Store a sufficient supply of expressed milk for the caregiver to use

- Become proficient at breast-feeding so that it's routine and easily manageable when you're working

If you want your baby to have only breast milk, prepare for the challenge of finding a good setting to express your milk during the day. Otherwise, you have to find a caregiver who is nearby and able to bring your baby to your work. A woman who works full time can expect to be away from her baby for up to ten hours, which equals two or three pumping sessions.

Overcoming the Challenges of Breast-Feeding While Working

As a working mother who is breast-feeding, you'll face a double challenge: how to implement an important personal commitment while maintaining your professional image. Even sympathetic, flexible employers will expect you to produce as much as before or to arrange for the objective to be met some other way. Try to face the task realistically:

- *Make arrangements in advance*—Don't assume that everyone will agree with your plans. Discuss the subject early, before you go on maternity leave. Evaluate your daily work schedule to find times when you will have the opportunity to nurse or express your milk. If you have to feed or express twice during your workday, you might suggest that your lunch hour be divided up or perhaps you could come in earlier or leave later to make up for your milk collection time.

Your boss may be reluctant, in which case you need to emphasize the potential benefits to the company: (1) a breast-fed baby is healthier; therefore, you will not need to miss as many days because of illness, and (2) a happier mother is a more productive worker.

Once you have approval, evaluate your daily work schedule to choose the best times when you will not be tense or rushed. Plan on a half an hour for a feeding or expressing; although expressing may be faster, it requires clean-up time.

• *Speak with your coworkers*—Always discuss your plans in advance to draw out any potential negative reactions. If they feel resentful because they have to take on some of your responsibilities, avoid getting defensive. Any inconvenience to them is temporary and they'll probably forget about it soon. Look for coworkers who have been or who are going through the experience and suggest forming a support group.

• *Consider bringing baby to work*—Under the proper conditions, this can be a good opportunity to visit with your baby during the day. Breast-feeding relaxes most women, after which they're eager to get back to work.

Other mothers, however, find that this option is just another painful separation and would prefer to avoid it. Some women enjoy keeping their babies with them throughout the workday, but such an arrangement puts extraordinary demands on a working mother and on colleagues. Nearby child care, if possible, can solve the problem of a long absence from baby.

Now that the basic decision has been made, it's time to arrange things in the office:

• *Protect your privacy*—This is important because you need to relax to allow your milk to flow freely. Pumping in an employee's lounge or a bathroom sometimes won't do. Instead, look for an empty office with a lock on the door (or use a Do Not Disturb sign), a supply closet, or a space in a health facility. As a last resort, use a conference room. Make sure there is an outlet for an electric pump, if you are using one, and a comfortable chair. You will also need a place to store your equipment during the day.

• *Appoint someone to run interference*—Ask a coworker nearby to stop anyone who is about to disturb you.

• *Arrange for a substitute*—Ask a coworker to fill in for you while you're breast-feeding or expressing with the understanding that you'll pay back the time when your baby is weaned.

• *Keep your expressed breast milk cool*—If no refrigerator is available at the office, bring an insulated cooler, filled with chill packs (refreezable, plastic containers of liquid), to store the milk. Relieve soreness by placing some cool compresses on your breasts. Or use a package of frozen peas or other vegetable as a quick substitute.

Dressing for Successful Breast-Feeding at Work

Wearing appropriate attire to work tells your employer and those you work with that you're serious about what you do and that you're dedicated to your job. That doesn't have to change when you become a nursing mother. It's still possible to appear professional, but it will take a little more effort.

Special fashions for the working nursing mother are available in many maternity shops, catalogs, and online retailers; however, you can also adapt your well-fitted, stylish clothes from the same wardrobe you usually wear. Just wear the ones that fit and fill in with some borrowed items. The following suggestions will help you maintain your appearance:

- *Use easy-care clothes*—Clothing that is washable and wrinkle-resistant is the best. Avoid solid colored tops and anything that is sheer. Brightly colored, printed tops will help camouflage milk stains if your full breasts leak, especially on days when meetings or presentations are scheduled.

- *Wear plastic breast shields*—They will help with leakage during these short periods of time. Wearing these shields for a long period of time can cause problems because of retained moisture on nipples (see "The

Leakage Problem," page 336). A simple black dress with a scarf or a large necklace may help divert attention away from the leaks.

• *Look for easily opened garments*—Wear blouses as well as knit pullovers and sweaters. Garments that open at the waist or button down the front can easily be lifted or pulled aside. Try the new nursing-print tank tops under your non-nursing garments. Some of the more popular access options include dual side panels (central slits), crop over top (dual slits), vest front (dual slit or extended arm holes), and central pleat (dual slits).

• *Keep a cover-up handy*—Have a nursing cape or a loose-fitting cardigan, for example, at your desk. And don't overlook the cover-up possibilities of ponchos, jackets, scarves, and receiving blankets. A vest with a shorter shirt underneath gives you a polished look and eliminates fabric bunches.

• *Wear a nursing bra*—Nursing bras come in lots of different styles, from plain to lacy, and in black, white, and ivory. They are usually sold in medium or firm support (for larger breasts). Sizing is the same as for ordinary bras. Buy your nursing bra towards the very end of your pregnancy; otherwise the fit will be wrong after the birth.

You'll need at least two or three nursing bras. Because you are constantly producing milk, you'll need to wash your bras frequently, even if you are using a breast pad to soak up the excess. Night time nursing bras are also available. They have all the design features of a nursing bra, but are lighter weight to wear.

A cotton nursing bra will support your heavier-than-usual breasts and help prevent sagging and stretch marks. The best ones have wide straps of fabric, and drop fronts for quick convenience. If the bra becomes too tight once your milk production is high, buy an extender found in department stores or in maternity shops. Small-breasted women may be able to get by with a stretch bra, which can be lifted up above the breast.

• *Use nursing pads*—Always have a good supply at hand. Place a pad on one side while your baby is feeding at the other. Wear them as a precautionary measure when you anticipate leaking. Change pads frequently, and wash them as soon as possible in hot, soapy water. Dry them thoroughly before using again. If you use disposable pads, avoid the plastic-coated ones, which might cause a rash, or wear the plastic side out. You can make your own pads from disposable diapers, sanitary napkins, cloth, or gauze.

The Leakage Problem

The disadvantage of having an excellent milk supply is the problem of leaking breasts. This usually occurs just prior to feeding or expressing time, but it may also happen when you're just thinking about your baby. A working woman has to be especially inventive to avoid embarrassment. Here are some measures you can take:

- *Stop the milk flow*—When you feel the familiar tingle associated with milk letdown (or ejection), press against your nipples to prevent leaking. Cross your arms and press the heel of your hand, or one finger, against the nipple. If you're sitting down, rest your chin in your hand and press your breast into your arm.

- *Keep extra supplies handy*—Keep at least one breast pad in your pocket and a few more in your purse and desk drawer. Use a cut-up diaper, handkerchief, or a sanitary pad in a pinch. Have an extra nursing bra at work in case one gets soaked. And don't forget to have a cover up or two.

FYI: Where to Go for Help with Breast-Feeding

Ask your pediatrician or childbirth instructor for help if you're having problems with feedings. Or contact your local La Leche League. Other helpful sources include the Red Cross, the YWCA, or a maternity center. There are books and videos that address this subject too. The International Board of Lactation Consultant Examiners certifies consultants who meet with clients, usually for a fee. Some insurance policies cover these consultations.

Guidelines While Traveling

During this breast-feeding period, it would be wise to avoid very lengthy business trips. They would have a negative effect on your milk supply and increase the difficulty of resuming a good feeding relationship with your baby on your return.

- *Out-of-town trips*—Some fortunate mothers can take their babies and caregiver with them when they travel. Most mothers, however, must leave their babies at home and express sufficient milk in advance to leave a good supply. If you're one of these working mothers, you'll have to travel with a breast pump to relieve your discomfort and, more importantly, to keep the milk flowing.

  You must allot sufficient time for expressing milk in an unhurried way. Try to pump as close to regular feeding times as possible. Because storing it would be next to impossible, this milk will probably be discarded. Nurse more frequently when you get home and your milk production should soon be back to normal.

- *Short trips*—If you will be bringing your baby along, prepare several chilled bottles of expressed milk for local trips of over three hours. Carry them in an insulated cooler with frozen chill packs. Individual foam soft drink can insulators or several layers of wet newspapers will do the trick at the last minute.

  Bring a thermos bottle filled with hot water for heating the milk. Simply pour hot water in the cup and set the bottle in it for several minutes. You can also use an electric bottle warmer that plugs directly into your cigarette lighter. Or bring measured amounts of formula powder and a thermos full of boiled water and combine them at feeding time. Ready-to-use, canned formula is another option. Take supplies with you—bottles, nipples, and a can opener—and just pour as you need it.

About the Author

Marla Schram Schwartz is the author of *Fairy Fun—A Craftivity Book for Children*; *Be a TV Game Show Winner!*, and coauthor of *The Bride Guide— The Perfect Wedding Planner*, now in its twenty-fifth year. She has also written greeting cards, cartoon gags, game concepts, and short stories.

In between mothering and writing, Marla volunteers for various elderly, poor, children, and animal humane groups. She also enjoys tennis, golf, yoga, and playing poker.

Marla Schram Schwartz lives in Westlake Village, California, with her nineteen-year-old daughter, Lindsey Erin; sixteen-year-old son, Brendan Taylor; seven-year-old standard poodle, Touchdown; and her husband of twenty-five years, Arnie.